Studying students

Studyin
A Second Look

Edited by

Nancy Fried Foster

Association of College and Research
A division of the American Library Association

Chicago 2013

The paper used in this publication meets the minimum requirements of American National Standard for Information Sciences–Permanence of Paper for Printed Library Materials, ANSI Z39.48-1992. ∞

Library of Congress Cataloging in Publication Control Number: 2013038851

Printed in the United States of America.

17 16 15 14 13   5 4 3 2 1

Contents

Acknowledgments

On behalf of the authors of these chapters, I would like to thank all of the librarians and library staff who have participated in numerous projects at the University of Rochester's River Campus Libraries. Over the past 10 years we have studied faculty member, graduate students, undergraduates, and even the staff of the library. These studies have been cumulative both in allowing us to develop a growing base of knowledge on which to build and in providing us time and room for growth as practitioners. Our methods are better now, and we are better at using them.

From the very beginning we have been inspired and informed by books and projects by a variety of anthropologists and librarians. The long list would include people who wrote ethnographies of higher education, such as Cathy Small, Dorothy Holland and Margaret Eisenhart, Susan Blum, Richard O'Connor, the late Michael Moffatt, and others who pioneered theory, such as Andrew Abbott, and methods, such as Douglas Harper. A number of people who also conduct work-practice studies and participatory design projects have been generous with time and ideas; they include Keith Webster, Michael Seadle, Birte Christensen-Dalsgaard, Merrilee Proffitt, Arnold Arcolio, Aradhana Goel, Nicole Hennig, Françoise Brun-Cottan, Pat Wall, Jennifer Englert, Brinda Dalal, and many others. We are also indebted to people whose work in other areas improved, and, in some cases, made our own work possible: Alice Bishop, Mike Roy, and our colleagues at many institutions, near and far, from Ithaca, Chicago, Columbus, and Cambridge, Massachusetts, to Paris, Rome, Beirut, Sharjah, and Bishkek. We wish we could name them all because everything we have done has been intertwined and dependent on the thought, creativity and effort of others.

Portions of the research discussed in this volume were made possible by grants from the Institute for Museum and Library Services and the Andrew W. Mellon Foundation, and we thank them for their generous support. Thanks from all of us to Ron Dow, Stanley Wilder, Susan Gibbons, and David Lindahl who made it possible for us to do this work and special thanks from me for the opportunity to become the project anthropologist. We thank them and Mary Ann Mavrinac who helped us see the project through to completion.

Several colleagues get our special thanks for the work they did on Undergraduate Research Refresher teams: Barbara Alvarez, Suzanne Bell, Marc Bollmann, Vicki Burns, Diane Cass, Bill Gavett, Kathy McGowan, Sean Morris, Harish Nayak, Katie Papas, and Nate Sarr. This book would still be on the drawing board were it not for Judi Briden's many extra efforts.

We are grateful to our publisher, Kathryn Deiss of the Association of College and Research Libraries, who makes everything so easy for us. Katie Palfreyman did a wonderful job of copyediting, and we thank ACRL's Senior Production Editor, Dawn Mueller, for her great design work.

Anyone who does projects like these knows that it is only through the voluntary participation of numerous students, faculty members, staff members, and other colleagues that a project like this is possible. Our participants remain anonymous but they have our deepest gratitude.

Finally, I thank my colleagues at the University of Rochester's River Campus Libraries for all of their hard work on these chapters and for almost 10 years of wonderful collaboration. Working with them has been a joy.

I dedicate this book to Robert Foster who makes me think and laugh.

Nancy Fried Foster
Rochester, New York
July 2013

chapter one. **Reporting on the Undergraduate Research Refresher**

Nancy Fried Foster

What do students really do when they receive an assignment to write a paper? What happens between receiving that assignment and handing something in? We asked those questions in a project we conducted in 2004 and 2005 at the University of Rochester's River Campus Libraries and described in the book we published two years later, *Studying Students: The Undergraduate Research Project at the University of Rochester*. We were surprised and gratified that so many people expressed interest in our project and the book and in the way we had incorporated anthropological methods into the design of library facilities, technologies, and services. Six years later, we still field inquiries about that project and people continue to download the book from our institutional repository.[1]

In recent years, we began to ask ourselves whether our undergraduates were still the same as they had been almost 10 years ago when we did the first study. Had anything changed about our undergraduates and their work practices? We also developed an interest in new topics, such as the study groups that had grown in importance in the last few years. Accordingly, we convened a team and conducted a new study, the Undergraduate Research Refresher, from 2011–2013. This book reports on the new study and draws comparisons to the original work.

A Second Volume

Readers of our first book will find that much is new here. Not only did we develop some new interests of our own, the librarians who approached us to ask about the book wanted to know what changes we had seen in the intervening years, and they wanted more information about our findings and how we acted on them. This book attempts to answer all of these questions.

In this volume, we give basic methodological information, but the focus is on what we learned and how we acted on it.

Where possible, we compare the data we collected in the earlier study to the more recent data to see what remained the same and what changed.

We replicated many of our original studies, including photo and retrospective interviews, map diaries, and our investigation of faculty expectations. But we added several new subprojects. These include a study of how new students "learn the ropes;" an investigation of how a variety of students, faculty members, and librarians find information that is personally important to them; an update on the technology use of our undergraduates and their professors; and a look at the study groups in which students participate by choice or assignment. Readers will find chapters on these topics, as well as on the more general re-studies.

As in our first study, we have taken care to report our findings in a way that preserves the anonymity of the students, staff, and faculty members who were kind enough to let us interview them. All our work is reviewed by the Institutional Review Board at the University of Rochester and team members who enroll subjects have taken ethics training. When we use student photos, we have permission to do so. In some chapters we use pseudonyms to refer to students and we have removed details from quoted material to prevent readers from identifying individuals.

In this Book

We start the book by asking what our faculty members expect of students. In Chapter 2, "Hallmarks of a Good Paper," Nora Dimmock reviews what faculty members deem to be a good research paper and what challenges they believe students face in doing good work on their papers. Building on work done in our first study, the chapter reveals that there is still a clear variation in expectations among teaching faculty. However, when we compare the expectations of faculty in the sciences, social sciences, and humanities, we see some patterns related to the importance of clarity of thought and expression. Furthermore, across all fields there is more concern than we expected with analysis and synthesis and less with the particular resources that students find and use. This being the case, Dimmock argues, our strategy of focusing on finding resources, rather than on using them, may be misguided. She writes that "faculty members are not dissatisfied at all with the role the library and librarians play in the production of student research," calling this "both a blessing and a curse." She goes on to make a case for building on what is working while pursuing some recent innovations that will help the library keep up with changes in scholarship and resulting changes in what students and scholars need from the library.

"An academic library needs to balance conservative and progressive forces to maintain relevance over time for an ever-changing student body," write Solomon Blaylock and Cynthia Carlton. In Chapter 3, "Discovering Undergraduate Technology Use," they review the activities of a team that studied student use of apps and devices to develop ideas for better library technology services. They were able to assess the extent to which students own and use mobile and other hi-tech devices and which ones they use for academic work as opposed to social activities. They also report the results of a design workshop in which students conveyed information about their academic work practices while developing blue-sky ideas for new apps to help them in their courses. "Nearly all students believe that technology or the web enhances their learning," they report, and their instructors often require that they use new technologies to complete course work. They conclude with a call for the library to be at the technological forefront, both to provide the best services and to establish credibility with the students whose needs the library seeks to address.

We know that students make heavy use of mobile devices, laptops, and associated apps, but that does not mean that they use only the latest technology. The tools students use range from pens and pencils and notebooks of the three-holed-lined variety to whiteboards to sophisticated lab equipment and statistical applications. Judi Briden and Sarada George explain a photo elicitation method in Chapter 4, "Picture My Work," that provides this insight and many others into the lives of our undergraduates. Following the work of a visual sociologist, Douglas Harper, we asked students to take a number of photographs for us such as their research tools, communication devices, favorite places to do their work, and even their favorite shoes. We asked students to talk to us about those photos in individual interviews and probed for information about how they do their academic work and how they manage this work in their full lives. Briden and George find some differences between the photos—and the lives—of students in our original study and the way they live and work now. Interestingly, the differences are less related to technology than to a new emphasis on group work, both voluntary and assigned. Illustrated with the images and the words of the students, this chapter provides information about how students decide which spaces to use for different kinds of academic work, the technologies they prefer, and their management of personal and academic relationships with peers. They argue the necessity of providing for a wide range of academic activities and for differences in how individuals work best.

That individuals work very differently is abundantly clear in Chapter 5, "Learning the Ropes," by Marcy Strong, Kenn Harper, and Mari Tsuchiya. We had noticed that students seemed strikingly different as seniors than they did when they entered as relatively "clueless" eighteen-year-olds. We had also seen evidence in our students' unfolding lives of a possible connection between a student's performance and his or her engagement and interest in some academic department or area of study. We wondered whether this was an accurate perception and, if so, what contributed to this change in our students and how it might affect the work of librarians. In this chapter, the authors explain the methods we used to test our ideas. They also review the findings, reflecting on the four mutually reinforcing ways in which our students mature: academic, social, emotional, and physical. Taking this further, they lay out steps librarians can take to support student maturation, especially engagement with academic opportunities and scholarly resources.

We know about faculty expectations of student research papers from Chapter 2 and learn in Chapter 3 that students and faculty members all use applications and devices heavily for personal and academic purposes. Chapter 4 tells us that they use a variety of high- and low-tech approaches to doing their work. We wondered what approach they take as they search for information in real life situations, and whether they do what their professors do when writing a research paper. In Chapter 6, "'Whatever Works:' Finding Trusted Information," Helen Anderson and Sarah Sexstone review a study of the research

processes used by faculty, students, and librarians and the implications of the findings for librarian practice. They identify an *ad hoc* approach to finding information that entails the use of any available tool and resource plus a critical ability built up through experience and study. They recommend ways in which an understanding of this "whatever works" method can be leveraged to help students write their papers.

Chapter 7, "Research as Connection," pursues many of the same themes as Chapter 6 through analyses of information from the Undergraduate Research Refresher and additional studies. Nancy Fried Foster begins by writing, "Our studies show that all researchers use a large number of means to get the information they need but no other means approaches the importance of consultation of each other." She argues that all serious researchers use a method in which questions drive the activation of a network of experts and the use of their ideas and writings. This method differs from approaches taught at the reference desk or in bibliographic instruction, and the author further argues that it may be possible to innovate better methods for instructing students by acknowledging and incorporating knowledge of the methods used by experienced researchers, whether they are faculty members, librarians, or even students.

Building on a groundwork laid in earlier chapters, Sarada George and Nancy Fried Foster write in Chapter 8 about "Understanding How Undergraduates Work." Consulting a range of data from many sub-studies, they focus on drawings students made of their paper-writing process in interviews conducted soon after a completed paper was submitted. The "retrospective" interviews during which students created their drawings trace all the steps from the assignment of the paper until it was handed in and include information about people the students consulted, the resources and technologies they used, and even the times and places of their work sessions. In the patterns that emerge from the interviews, we see that the overall writing process has remained fairly stable over the years since the first study, but some things have changed. For example, students in 2011 carried laptops around with them much more than in 2005, and they had access to many more course materials online through Blackboard and other applications. In general, the authors report that the availability of online resources had increased exponentially and yet many students still used paper for reading and for writing in the later study. The data suggest that the keys to good paper writing lie in the students' ability to connect to what they are studying.

As online resources boom, and even though many students still like books, we might well ask whether traditional academic libraries will continue to meet our students' needs and, if not, how we should change them. This is the central question of Chapter 9, "Designing Academic Libraries with the People Who Work in Them," by Nancy Fried Foster. The chapter opens with the words of David Cronrath, the dean of the University of Maryland's School of Architecture, Planning & Preservation: "In unstable times a physical re-programming can no longer depend on traditional, professional experts (architects and librarians), for whom precedent is now unreliable." The chapter then starts with a review of guides to the design of academic libraries, tracing the appearance of participatory or user-centered processes. Several library renovation projects are described to illustrate the evolution of a participatory approach to design at the University of Rochester's River Campus Libraries. The chapter concludes with a call for the use of participatory processes to envisage the future of academic libraries.

In Chapter 10, "Study Groups in Libraries: Exponential Benefits," Alison Bersani, Judi Briden, Sue Cardinal, and Katie Clark describe research we did on students who, voluntarily or not, work on assignments or study for examinations in groups. In interviews with a variety of study groups, the team identified many motivations and approaches. They also found reasons to wonder whether and when group study is actually advantageous but concluded that many study groups help students focus, share information, fill in each other's learning gaps, reinforce the material, and develop skill in working cooperatively. They propose ways the library can support group work with improvements to resources, services, or facilities.

This volume concludes with Chapter 11, "Where Do We Go From Here?," a meditation on what we have learned and how we can apply our new knowledge. In this chapter, Solomon Blaylock, Judi Briden, and LeRoy LaFleur begin by stressing the importance of understanding the whole student and then seeing how the library and other resources arrayed around students fit into their practices. They make a convincing case for seeing libraries from the perspective of students, as a place that is "right" for the serious and focused work of learning and for building community. The authors provide guidance on what librarians and faculty members can do to act on what we have learned.

Participatory Design in Libraries: Past and Prospect

Many people have asked how we came to employ an anthropologist and use ethnographic methods in library design at the University of Rochester. David Lindahl had worked as a computer scientist on a multi-disciplinary R&D team at Xerox and Xerox PARC. He found the combination of technologists, designers, and ethnographers to be extremely effective in technology design. Lindahl came to the River Campus Libraries as the webmaster where he joined forces with Susan Gibbons, who was then working on an e-book project. Gibbons' approach to developing library technologies and services was innovative, user-centered, and based on asking people about their work rather than assuming that she already knew what they needed. The two of them jointly managed the Digital Initiatives Unit, a unit they had begun to expand with the addition of a developer and a graphic designer. Next they wanted to add an anthropologist; Stanley Wilder, the associate dean, encouraged them to get a grant to pilot that idea. Gibbons and Lindahl secured funding from the Institute for Museum and Library Services for a project to study the creation and use of grey literature by faculty members and the development of new DSpace functionality to meet faculty needs in connection with grey literature. When the grant came through, they hired an anthropologist, Nancy Fried Foster, to facilitate the project.

From that very first project, the team experienced many successes: in connecting with faculty, students and staff; in developing better interfaces and software applications; in improving services; and in renovating library spaces to meet needs we only learned about through our projects.

We have been almost overwhelmed at the reception to our work at conferences, on campus visits, in the response to our first book, and in the role our implementations have played—sometimes by example and sometimes just by provocation—in moving libraries forward in these turbulent times. It has been especially gratifying that librarians at other institutions have used our methods and developed their own methods, which we, in turn, have emulated. There is now a community of librarians who use a participatory design approach or incorporate user research into their decision making, design, and usability testing protocols.

As our team has changed, with people arriving and others leaving, we might have wondered whether our approach would endure, but the health of our cross-institutional community provides reassurance. Participatory design and user research are now practiced by enough people that they will remain in the toolkit—to be used when they are needed, for some time to come.

Our hope is that readers of this book will consider using the methods at their own institutions and becoming part of our community of librarians and library technologists. We encourage our readers to talk with the people who use library collections, services, and facilities and to continue to share what they learn with each other for the benefit of libraries everywhere.

Notes

1. *Studying Students: The Undergraduate Research Project at the University of Rochester* is available as a free download at http://hdl.handle.net/1802/7520 and in print or as e-book at: http://www.alastore.ala.org/detail.aspx?ID=2322.

chapter two. **Hallmarks of a Good Paper**

Nora Dimmock

In our original undergraduate research study, we interviewed faculty members in an attempt to discover what they considered the hallmarks of a good research paper. We found that there was very little agreement among them as to what defines a good paper, especially across the disciplines (Alvarez & Dimmock, 2007, p. 4). There was some agreement that well-written research papers used appropriate resources, were structurally sound, well developed, and demonstrated critical engagement with the subject. There was more general agreement, however, about what faculty members saw as obstacles to good writing, many of them characterized by the word "poor:" "poor time management skills, poor understanding of the material, poor writing skills … and poor choice of topic and lack of focus" (Alvarez & Dimmock, 2007,p. 3). Our motivation in embarking on the original study was to see whether a deeper understanding of faculty expectations might make it possible for librarians to help students become more accomplished researchers. We learned that part of the solution lay in helping students become better writers, and a stronger partnership with the college writing center emerged as one outcome of our original project. We also saw a role for ourselves in bridging the gap between students and faculty members. That is, by involving ourselves in all phases of the curriculum through increased outreach, we found we could help students understand faculty expectations, do better research, and write better papers.

We had several reasons for revisiting this research, but most importantly we wanted to see whether faculty expectations had changed since the original interviews. We surmised that even if they had not, the interviews would still serve as an excellent outreach tool for librarians and provide some benefit to students. Another motivation was to see if the College of Arts, Science, and Engineering's emphasis on undergraduate research was having any effect on faculty expectations of scholarly writing and other forms of scholarly communication. If so, was there a new role for librarians in the research enterprise? Finally, our rationale for repeating many of the studies in our original Undergraduate Research project was simply that we have evolved into a responsive learning community that continually seeks feedback to ensure that our current practice is aligned with the teaching and research mission of the University.

Information Literacy and Faculty Expectations

Several studies of faculty expectations have been published since we conducted faculty interviews in 2005 and 2006. Many of these studies were focused on faculty perceptions of information literacy (IL) as defined by the Association of College and Research Libraries' (ACRL) "Information Literacy Competency Standards for Higher Education" (ACRL, 2000; Gullikson, 2006; McGuinness, 2006). Information literacy, as defined by the ACRL, is the ability to locate, use, and manage information effectively and appropriately in order to become a "lifelong learner." Supporters of formal institutionalized information literacy programs within higher education argue that the library is uniquely positioned to fulfill this educational role that is critical to students' academic success. In fact, establishing an information literacy curriculum in the library outside of the academic disciplines is one approach that many colleges and universities have taken. However, this assumes a library-centric curriculum contrary to ACRL's standards' recommended best practices, which call for embedding IL skills in the disciplines throughout the program of study by means of librarian-faculty collaboration (Gullikson, 2006, p. 583). Gullikson (2006) found little guidance in the existing literature to help librarians succeed at the uncomfortable task of "work[ing] with faculty to integrate our standards into their curriculum" (p. 584). In 2005, the author surveyed faculty in all disciplines at four Canadian universities, asking them to rank the importance of the specific outcomes in the standards and to indicate the academic level at which they expected students to display those skills. In most cases, Gullikson found that all participating faculty concurred on the ten highest-rated outcomes, which included outcomes from all five of the standards. These included locating appropriate resources, citing them correctly, evaluating them critically, integrating them effectively, and so on. There was less agreement among faculty about the academic level at which students should acquire the skills; however, the fact that faculty and librarians agreed on the importance of the skills for student success demonstrated that the standards could provide a common ground for collaboration.

McGuinness (2006) attempted to discover the factors in an academic environment that can interfere with faculty-librarian collaboration in information literacy development by conducting semi-structured interviews with sociology and civil engineering faculty to determine their beliefs and expectations. Most faculty participants believed that students become information literate by researching, writing, and presenting the assignments in their courses. In other words, they assumed that students learn by doing, often by working with their fellow students. Many believed that students who have personal interests in subjects are motivated to develop the literacy skills they need and that they eventually succeed using "trial and error" methods. Consequently, faculty tended to assume that no formal instruction is needed in the curriculum to enable students to develop competence, leading the author to conclude that formal information literacy skill-building had not become a priority for faculty. In another study, DaCosta (2010) surveyed higher education faculty in England and the United States to determine how they perceive information literacy and whether they help students develop information literacy skills in their courses. The findings were similar across the two countries with respect to faculty perceptions of the importance of the skills and their use of information skills in the curricula. Most faculty respondents want students to acquire the skills, but only about half are teaching or assessing the development of those skills. Fewer than half of the faculty believed that students actually acquire the skills by the end of their degree programs.

Writing Better in the Disciplines

In addition to research centered on how faculty expect students to find and use appropriate information, several researchers have looked at how faculty help students develop the skills they need to write successful research papers (Baglione, 2008; Reynolds, Smith, Moskovitz, & Sayle, 2009). In "Doing Good and Doing Well: Teaching Research-Paper Writing by Unpacking the Paper," author Baglione (2008) notes, "good writing, then, is simply more than proper grammar, usage, and paragraph construction; it embodies the conventions, values, and norms of the discipline for which it is written" (p. 595). The author sees teaching students how to write an effective research paper as exclusively the faculty member's responsibility and even in the section on locating resources sees no role for the librarian. Reynolds, Smith, Moskovitz, & Sayle (2009) found the increased emphasis on undergraduate research and capstone projects in the scientific disciplines created the need for more formalized support structures for students writing an undergraduate thesis. The authors created a rubric, the Biology Thesis Assessment Protocol (BioTAP), for the biology department at Duke University to address faculty members' perceived gap between student writing skills and departmental expectations of writing quality. "For students, BioTAP promotes the development of writing and critical-thinking skills by clearly communicating the expectations for the thesis, and by teaching students how to respond to and solicit useful feedback on their writing to guide the revision process" (Reynolds et al., p. 897). The BioTAP instrument has a number of milestones built into its design, including several stages of revision and feedback based on the disciplinary peer review process, giving it an added value for providing professional experience.

Experiential Learning and Undergraduate Research

The push for experiential learning and for engaging undergraduates in the research enterprise of higher education is another theme in the literature relevant to faculty expectations of student research. The shift to "a user-centered approach" (MacMillan, 2009, p. 133) presents a new opportunity for faculty-librarian partnerships that create "learning activities and authentic assignments that mirror professional tasks" (p.135). Through systematic assessment, MacMillan studied undergraduate journalism majors over a five-year span in an effort to uncover not only how they find and use information, that is, how they learn information literacy skills, but more broadly, how students learn best. One finding was that students use a much broader range of tools and strategies than librarians do, highlighting the need for librarians to assess their own

skill set periodically to remain relevant. McClellen and Hyle's (2012) study of the experiential learning experiences of college students engaged in qualitative research points out that "the goal of higher education should be to facilitate learning through experience" (p. 240). Their study highlights the importance of collaboration and teamwork in the research process, and the value of what they term "the importance of the unfamiliar context" (McClellan & Hyle, p. 250): being forced to see things differently by stepping outside the familiar. "All of us (faculty and students) became more skillful in research techniques—the obvious intended outcome. But we also became more self-reflexive and aware of our own positions within complex, and often foreign, contexts" (McClellan & Hyle, 2012, p. 250).

Stamatoplos (2009) calls for an expanded service model for academic librarianship to support an expanded definition of undergraduate research. "Because it is an experiential form of learning, campuses are recognizing undergraduate research as an important recruitment and retention tool" (Stamatoplos, 2009, p. 235). The author notes that the type of research faculty members and students do outside the classroom actually presents a larger role for librarian collaboration than the current model whereby librarians assist students in finding resources for research assignments embedded in the curriculum. At Indiana University–Purdue University Indianapolis, academic librarians were part of the team that established the Undergraduate Research Opportunity Program (UROP) and have been integral to its success. Through their collaboration with faculty and undergraduate researchers, librarians have discovered that there is a real difference in the information-seeking activities and behaviors of students when they are engaged in disciplinary research as opposed to researching for class assignments. The disconnect between how librarians teach students to find resources and how researchers in the disciplines actually do their research was the subject of a paper presented at the ACRL Library Assessment Conference in 2010: "The Librarian-Student-Faculty Triangle: Conflicting Research Strategies?" (Foster, 2010). Foster (2010) found "evidence in our research at the University of Rochester of a clash between the library-based research practices of productive scholars, on the one hand, and the services delivered at the reference desk or in bibliographic instruction, on the other" (p. 1). One major difference between the way librarians and scholars do research involves the organization of resources and how they are gathered within the research process: Librarians build a broad and complex set of resources that cover all the possibilities, while researchers build a more deliberate and targeted set of resources based on disciplinary practice. She concluded that undergraduate students would benefit from working with librarians whose instruction strategies and research methods were more in sync with their professors.[1]

Methodology

In our 2011 study, we followed a similar methodology as our first study by having subject librarians interview faculty members who had recently assigned and graded a research paper. In the first study, we interviewed 12 faculty members, including six from the social sciences, four from the humanities, and two from science disciplines. Several faculty members in that initial study noted that one of the hallmarks of a good paper was correct disciplinary style, so for this study we decided to change our methodology to add a disciplinary focus. Twenty interviews were conducted in 2011, including eight in the social sciences, seven in the humanities, and five in science disciplines. We also slightly altered our interview questions (see Appendix 2B) to elicit a more critical response. Interviews were recorded and transcribed for analysis. In addi-

tion, the librarians conducting the interviews were asked to take notes, which were included with the transcriptions.

The first step in data analysis involved bringing together three teams of librarians, representing the social sciences, the humanities, and the sciences, respectively, to develop and summarize a comparison of findings across the disciplines. We accomplished this through a simple thematic encoding technique by which each team member reads through his or her assigned transcripts and notes, distilling key information onto Post-It notes. We then categorized and aggregated the Post-Its to find trends in the data, including findings specific to the role of librarians in helping students write good research papers. (See Appendix 2C for the results of this exercise.)

Discussion

Changing our methodology to focus on disciplinary similarities and differences revealed more detail about what faculty members consider important to success in undergraduate writing. As the table in Appendix 2A shows, while there was considerable variation from one faculty member to another, responses within disciplinary areas showed a degree of consistency.

In the humanities and social sciences, faculty members noted that critical engagement with the subject and the sources was essential to good writing, whereas the sciences faculty noted good structure, strong writing, and logical flow as most important. Humanities faculty members cited clarity of argument as a hallmark of a good paper, while science faculty members cited clarity of thinking, which may not mean the same thing in a disciplinary context.

All three disciplines agreed that poor writing skills and summarizing sources instead of synthesizing them were problems. All three disciplines were also in general agreement that students were finding appropriate resources for their research, although the majority of the faculty members were unsure about how the students were finding these sources. Faculty members in all three disciplines agreed that students should be asking a subject librarian for help in locating appropriate resources as well as searching databases and browsing the stacks. But there were also some disciplinary differences in what the faculty members perceived to be the barriers to good writing, including lack of a logical framework (science), lack of engagement (humanities), and not following the directions of the assignment (social sciences).

In the course of our analysis, we found some disconnects between librarians and faculty members, especially with regard to the appropriateness of resources and proper citation. While faculty members did not indicate significant concern over the number or appropriateness of resources in student papers, librarians persisted in our discussions in claiming just the opposite. Librarians repeatedly focused on sources as both a problem and solution, commenting, "show students how to browse for books," "students don't understand the critical role of sources in the quality of the books," and so on. On other topics, librarians felt that there was just not enough specific information in the data to connect with their individual professional practice. This led to a discussion of how to improve the protocol for future faculty interviews. Should we repeat this project, we will collect and analyze assignments, ask more pointed questions about the writing process, determine whether there was any formal library involvement in the curriculum, ask for clarification for terms like "effort," and so on.

As liaisons to their academic departments, subject librarians often limit their service model to providing bibliographic services to faculty and graduate students in their disciplines. While this core activity is essential to the library's role in supporting teaching, research, and the production of scholarly communication, it can limit librarian-faculty collaboration. Librarians can be reluctant to approach faculty members

with ideas for bibliographic instruction or with feedback on student interactions at the reference desk. Faculty members may take librarian support for granted and assume that students are seeking out librarians on their own. A number of studies have looked at the faculty-librarian relationship in an effort to provide both communities common ground for improvement. Gunawardena, Weber, and Agosto (2010) define collaboration as "human behavior that makes a substantial contribution toward the advancement of a research project throughout its duration or for a large part of it, with respect to a mutually shared superordinate research goal and which takes place in a research setting" (p. 214). They note that faculty and librarians have divergent vocabularies, disciplinary paradigms, and perspectives on the meaning of collaboration and that this can affect meaningful partnerships. Christiansen, Stombler, and Thaxton (2004) conducted a sociological analysis of librarian-faculty relations through a literature review and found a symmetrical disconnect between the perceptions of both groups, but noted that only the librarians characterized the faculty-librarian relationship as problematic. The authors posit a two-sided knowledge literacy gap: Faculty think librarians lack the specific disciplinary expertise needed to select appropriate materials for a course or research project; librarians think faculty lack information literacy skills and have poor search techniques. Efforts to build collaborative relationships through bibliographic instruction, shared collection development, and other typical faculty-librarian interactions resulted in faculty members seeing librarians as professionals rather than fellow academics. Furthermore, the authors note that the proliferation of the library liaison model led faculty members to see their subject librarians as the go-to people for library problems, further distancing them from approaching each other from a position of true collaboration characterized by shared curricular goals.

Conclusion

Our original project sought to answer a question, "What are the hallmarks of a good research paper?" and discover what role the library and subject librarians play in the production of students' scholarly research. The findings suggested that we might want to take a more disciplinary focus for future research, so we repeated the study with that objective in mind. The overarching goal of both studies, however, was to inform our practice by hearing first-hand from faculty members their expectations of scholarly research and writing at the undergraduate level and to use that information to help students become more accomplished researchers and write better papers. As with our first study, we discovered that faculty members were generally satisfied with the sources students were using and that most of the obstacles to producing good research papers involved poor writing skills, not being able to make a good argument, summarizing rather than synthesizing sources, lack of critical thinking skills, and so on. None of these problems can be addressed with our usual bag of library tricks, such as bibliographic instruction, one-on-one research consultations, or reference desk interactions.

In fact, according to our studies, faculty members are not dissatisfied at all with the role the library and librarians play in the production of student research, which is both a blessing and a curse. The blessing is that we can confidently continue to do what we have been doing without causing the students or faculty any harm. The curse is that if we continue in a passive stance, we risk marginalizing both ourselves and the library in a future of scholarly research and communication that calls for a more active, collaborative, and substantial role for librarians in the production of knowledge.

Focusing on information literacy as a skill set outside of any discipline may further deepen the divide between librarians and faculty members and may sustain faculty members' assumptions that students are either consulting librarians or, in some other ineffable way, finding the research resources they need. For this reason, the one-shot bibliographic instruction session might not be the best course of action for subject librarians attempting to establish a collaborative relationship with faculty members in their disciplines.

Alternatively, subject librarians could be proactive in developing long-term collaborative relationships with faculty members through research projects that establish confidence and trust in the librarian's mastery of disciplinary research methods. Further collaboration could then be built on this framework of shared curricular goals, and the librarian might eventually be invited to collaborate as a full partner in creating the research assignment. The increased emphasis on undergraduate research provides subject librarians an excellent rationale for developing a new and expanded role in the research enterprise by joining individual and interdisciplinary research teams. As a department that spans the disciplines, the academic library can be both a conduit and bridge between disciplines engaged in new forms of scholarship and research. The emphasis on experiential learning may also provide new opportunities for librarian-faculty collaboration that may take the form of embedded reference, grant writing, fieldwork, and support for new modes of scholarly communication.

At the University of Rochester, two faculty-library collaborations have developed long-term projects that have expanded the subject librarian role to include instruction, curriculum development, and long-term academic planning. The Seward Family Papers project, led by history professor Thomas P. Slaughter, is one example of a successful collaboration that has had the added benefit of allowing library departments to work together. Under the direction of Dr. Slaughter, Lori Birrell, a manuscript librarian; Melissa Mead, a university archivist and digital media specialist; and Nora Dimmock, director of the Digital Humanities Center (DHC), all work within a disciplinary framework—characterized by new scholarly practices in historical editing sanctioned by the disciplinary authorities (American Historical Society)—to create an online scholarly edition of the Seward Family Papers. Students are transcribing letters from the collection housed in the Libraries' Department of Rare Books, Special Collections, and Preservation (RBSCP) and designing and building a technological framework for a scholarly online edition in collaboration with the DHC. In another collaboration, the DHC is working with English Professor Joel Burges and his students in a course called "The Poetics of Television" to visualize the temporal narrative structure of different television genres (sitcoms, miniseries, soap operas, and so on). In this project, Dimmock is a full collaborator in the design of the Humanities Lab curriculum. Future collaborations include a new course on mapping cultural spaces, which is being co-designed by modern languages and cultures librarian Kristen Totleben, German Professor June Hwang, and Dimmock.

Changing the role of subject librarians from tangential helpers to full collaborators in the research process will yield great rewards for our students, our faculty members, and ourselves. Adopting search strategies aligned with our disciplinary departments is one way to bridge the gap between student work and faculty expectations. For a library with a rich history in conducting user research, finding out the best way to make this a reality will be easy: Continue to ask the tough questions about what is and is not working and analyze the answers to determine how we can improve our practice to close the gap. The library can then be poised to seize emerging opportunities for collaboration and play an integral role in research and writing at every level.

Appendix 2A. Questions and Summary Responses by Discipline

Question 1: Thinking about these recent papers, what were the hallmarks of the best ones? What was it about the better papers that made them better?		
Science	**Social Science**	**Humanities**
Good structure Strong writing Logical flow Clarity of thinking	More effort Well written Critical, analytic Creative, original ideas Well-organized Good choice of topic Engaged, enthusiastic Good sources, well-cited Well-read, understand the literature Met assignment goals	Students are engaged critically with a subject and sources Clarity of argument Analyzed rather than summarized

Question 2: On this recent batch of papers, what were the biggest problems in the less successful research papers? What do you think were the obstacles in the way of students writing better papers?		
Science	**Social Science**	**Humanities**
Sentences/ideas were not well connected Lack of a logical framework Poor writing skills Student just summarized sources	Lack of effort Poor time management Plagiarism, cribbing Poor writing skills Lack of critical thinking Poor quality sources Not understanding the reading No original thinking Not following assignment directions	Not engaged Generalizing—summarizing Writing skills Unable to make an argument

Question 3: Thinking back on these papers, would you say that the resources students found and cited were appropriate and sufficient in most cases? Or do you think that this was one of the things that separated the good papers from the ones that were lacking?		
Science	**Social Science**	**Humanities**
Sources were mostly appropriate	Random sources from Internet Appropriate but not sufficient First sources found rather than best	Not a problem for all Better sources= better paper

Question 4: Do you have any sense of how students actually found resources—books, articles, or other information—for this recent batch of papers?		
Science	**Social Science**	**Humanities**
Instructor guides and suggests resources Do not know	Do not know Google, Internet Prof gave them sources Asked librarian Annotated bibliographies Databases	Do not know Bibliographic instruction Google Assigned resources Subject librarians

Question 5: Now, could I ask what you think they should be doing when they look for books, articles and other resources?		
Science	**Social Science**	**Humanities**
Wikipedia is a good start Searching Pubmed and Google Scholar Talking to a librarian	Should know how to do already Meet with faculty, librarian, writing center Use Voyager catalog	Subject librarians Browse the stacks Use databases Ask a librarian

Appendix 2B. Comparison of Interview Questions from 2007 and 2011 Studies

2007 Study Questions	2011 Study Questions
	I am going to ask you about the research papers that your students wrote earlier this semester for your course [number, name], and that you have graded. We'll keep talking about this recent batch of papers.
You are getting some research papers handed in within a few weeks. When you get these papers, what will you look for as the hallmarks of a good research paper?	Thinking about these recent papers, what were the hallmarks of the best ones? What was it about the better papers that made them better?
How do you expect students in this class to find books and articles for the research paper? (Probe: Materials given to them by professor? Expect students to find everything on their own? Expect students to seek out help from peers? Librarians? Others—who?	Thinking back on these papers, would you say that the resources students found and cited were appropriate and sufficient in most cases? Or do you think that this was one of the things that separated the good papers from the ones that were lacking? Do you have any sense of how students actually found resources—books, articles, or other information—for this recent batch of papers? Now, could I ask what you think they **should be** doing when they look for books, articles and other resources? (Probe: Expect students to find everything on their own? Expect students to seek out help from professor? From peers? Librarians? Others—who?)
What is the most helpful thing that I or the librarians at the reference desk can be doing right now to help your students finish this paper?	What is the most helpful thing that I or the librarians at the reference desk can be doing right now to help your students do a great job on their next paper?
Think about the research papers you got in some recent semester. What was the biggest obstacle to students writing successful research papers? (Probe: What about finding good books and articles—was that one of the major obstacles?) [If the answer to #4 has already come up in previous answers, you do not have to ask.]	On this recent batch of papers, what were the biggest problems in the less successful research papers? What do you think were the obstacles in the way of students writing better papers?
	Is there anything else I should know about this?

Appendix 2C. Summary Findings from Post-It Note Exercise

Issues Related to Librarian Role

- Show students how to browse for books
- Books—students aren't, don't, won't use books
- Get students into the stacks
- Students don't understand the critical role of sources in the quality of books
- What to with the challenge of not grading for the quality of sources?
- It is interesting that (some) faculty don't have an answer to what students should be doing to find sources
- Contradiction? Sources were fine, better papers better sources
- Critical thinking—where does the library fit
- Help students filter information
- Raise awareness of what library can do
- Help students learn how to ask questions

Notes

1. For further discussion of the research processes used by faculty members, librarians, and students, see Chapters 6, "'Whatever Works:' Finding Trusted Information," and 7, "Research as Connection."

References

Alvarez, B. & Dimmock, N. (2007). Faculty expectations of student research. In N. F. Foster & S. Gibbons (Eds.), *Studying students: The undergraduate research project at the University of Rochester* (pp. 1–6). Chicago, IL: Association of College and Research Libraries.

Association of College and Research Libraries. (2000). *Information literacy competency standards for higher education.* Retrieved from http://www.ala.org/acrl/sites/ala.org.acrl/files/content/standards/standards.pdf

Baglione, L. (2008). Doing good and doing well: Teaching research-paper writing by unpacking the paper. PS: Political Science & Politics, 41(3), 595–602. doi: http://dx.doi.org/10.1017/S1049096508080803

Christiansen, L., Stombler, M., & Thaxton, L. (2004). A report on librarian-faculty relations from a sociological perspective. *The Journal of Academic Librarianship, 30*(2), 116–121. doi: 10.1016/j.acalib.2004.01.003

DaCosta, J. W. (2010). Is there an information literacy skills gap to be bridged? An examination of faculty perceptions and activities relating to information literacy in the United States and England. *College & Research Libraries, 71*(3), 203–222. Retrieved from http://crl.acrl.org/content/71/3/203.full.pdf+html

Foster, N. F. (2010, October). The librarian-student-faculty triangle: Conflicting research strategies? Paper presented at the Association of Research Libraries' Annual Library Assessment Conference, Baltimore, MD. Retrieved from http://hdl.handle.net/1802/13512

Gullikson, S. (2006). Faculty perceptions of ACRL's information literacy competency standards for higher education. *The Journal of Academic Librarianship, 32*(6), 583–592. doi: 10.1016/j.acalib.2006.06.001

Gunawardena, S., Weber, R., & Agosto, D. E. (2010). Finding that special someone: Interdisciplinary collaboration in an academic context. *Journal of Education for Library and Information Science, 51*(4), 210–221. Retrieved from http://search.proquest.com/docview/759962938?accountid=13567

MacMillan, M. (2009). Watching learning happen: Results of a longitudinal study of journalism students. *The Journal of Academic Librarianship, 35*(2), 132–142. doi: 10.1016/j.acalib.2009.01.002

McClellan, R., & Hyle, A. E. (2012). Experiential learning: Dissolving classroom and research borders. *Journal of Experiential Education, 35*(1), 238–252. doi: 10.5193/JEE35.1.238

McGuinness, C. (2006). What faculty think–Exploring the barriers to information literacy development in undergraduate education. *The Journal of Academic Librarianship, 32*(6), 573–582. doi: http://dx.doi.org/10.1016/j.acalib.2006.06.002

Reynolds, J., Smith, R., Moskovitz, C., & Sayle, A. (2009). BioTAP: A systematic approach to teaching scientific writing and evaluating undergraduate theses. *Bioscience, 59*(10), 896–903. doi: http://dx.doi.org/10.1525/bio.2009.59.10.11

Stamatoplos, A. (2009). The role of academic libraries in mentored undergraduate research: A model of engagement in the academic community. *College & Research Libraries, 70*(3), 235–249. Retrieved from http://crl.acrl.org/content/70/3/235.full.pdf+html

chapter three. Discovering Undergraduate Technology Use

Solomon Blaylock and Cynthia Carlton

An academic library needs to balance conservative and progressive forces to maintain relevance over time for an ever-changing student body. Libraries serve as storehouses for the knowledge of past and current generations and provide an environment where the knowledge of the future may be formulated. The means by which that accumulated knowledge is accessed continue to change in the wake of innovations in information technology. The engaged academic library must monitor global technology trends as well as local technology adoption to develop new ideas and discover opportunities for new or refreshed innovative services that will support 21st-century learning.

When the University of Rochester's River Campus Libraries launched a re-study of undergraduates, we wanted to investigate the implications of changes in technology. We created the Applications and Devices sub-team to answer three questions: [1]

1. How can we assess student use of applications and devices?
2. How can we compare student use with that of faculty?
3. How can we use this information to help students effectively employ technology to connect with the best possible resources for their coursework and research and make the most of their educational opportunities?

Over the course of nine months, our sub-team conducted surveys and held face-to-face interviews about technology use with students and faculty members; analyzed information culled from large-scale undergraduate technology surveys conducted by University IT, which bookended our research; and hosted a design workshop for undergraduates and graduate students centered on the use of mobile devices and applications. [2] What we learned helped us understand the ways our student body makes use of technology and how we can begin to use this data to identify opportunities for improved services.

Methodology

Since we have a variety of information needs and several different student and faculty groups to reach, we developed a set of information gathering activities that comprised surveys, interviews, and a design workshop.

Student Interviews

For the first round of student interviews we sat down face-to-face with nine undergraduate students and asked a series of questions relating to what tech devices they owned, how frequently they used each and for what purpose, and what devices they planned to purchase in the near future. Potential participants were approached at random at a Starbucks on campus and offered a free coffee drink of their choice for their help. Interviews were recorded in a conference room upstairs from the café.

Faculty Survey and Interviews

A month later, our sub-team administered an online survey through SurveyMonkey, an online survey tool, to 23 faculty members; the survey dealt with personal and professional technology ownership and use. We followed up with face-to-face interviews of the five participants who agreed to help, in their respective offices, at their convenience.

Design Workshop

Subsequently, the Applications and Devices and Design Workshop sub-teams worked together to plan and conduct a design workshop focused on the development of a mobile app created to facilitate the writing of a research paper or the work of a study group. Volunteers were solicited by means of flyers posted around campus, which offered $20 and free snacks and drinks for the first 10 student volunteers who owned and were already familiar with the use of a smart phone, iPad, or iPod Touch. The ten students were quickly scheduled, a combination of undergraduate and graduate students. For this workshop, we knew we wanted to engage students in a conversation about applications on their smart phones. As already noted, a requirement of the workshop was that each student had to own a smart phone or an equivalent device, such as the iPod Touch. This would ensure that each participant had prior experience using this kind of technology and the apps that run on them.

Participants completed a written survey (an early version of the Winter 2010 Student Mobile Devices and Website Survey outlined later in this chapter) and took part in an energetic icebreaker exercise. For the warm-up exercise, we decided to try an idea that would not only be creative but relevant to the workshop and popular culture at the time. We had students create a live-action Angry Birds game. The Angry Birds game had been released for about a year and was popular among all age groups. The game centers on a group of birds that slingshot themselves into a structure in attempts to knock it down and destroy the pigs that are located inside. For our live-action Angry Birds game, we collected a variety of materials to build the structure: paper towel tubes, foam,

cardboard, small boxes, and cups. We purchased some ping-pong balls, painted them green, and attached some stickers for the eyes to represent the pigs. Then we collected several balls in varying size and weight to represent the birds. We split the workshop participants into two teams, and each had to build a structure and place the "pigs" inside. The teams then had to first knock down their own structure; set things back up; and then knock down the other team's structure. This got things rolling nicely.

Figure 3.1. Artifacts from the opening activity (Photo by Marc Bollman)

Next the students engaged in a brainstorming session. We presented them with two mobile application concepts: one that would simplify the writing of a research paper and one that would assist with the work of a study group. The students were encouraged to brainstorm ideas related to either application. Over the course of about 30 minutes, students produced 38 technology ideas, including applications or devices that would make communication and collaboration easier; capture notes from a whiteboard; translate; and help with formatting, citing, and avoiding plagiarism. They produced additional ideas for resources, including news and map resources; access to exemplary papers; dictionaries; and databases related to research topics. Students also produced ideas related to an app that could help them find groups and group spaces. Many of the ideas seemed challenging to produce given the current state of technology but might be feasible in coming years. One idea seemed completely impossible but summarized a lot of the other ideas: a "third brain."

Participants then broke into smaller groups to create a mockup of either application, conceptually and visually. Afterwards they presented their ideas to the reassembled group. Participation was enthusiastic and sustained; even students who initially appeared shy and reserved eventually became very vocal in their contributions. Interestingly, far more students chose to focus on the application related to study groups than that for writing a paper in the brainstorming portion of the workshop, and all of them did so during the development portion.

It was clear that students are highly motivated and interested to come up with ideas for making study groups better and easier to find. They easily dream up technologies that support the actual work of the group. Finally, they would also like technologies that help them find people so they can form a group or find an existing group they can join or just plain locate.

Following the workshop, sub-team members created ideas for apps that built on the analyses of information gathered from students. These concepts included the following:

- A branded version of Google Docs (now known as Google Drive)

- A variety of apps to broadcast study group locations and to help others establish their own study group, find an existing group, gather resources for groups study, run a study group, and so on
- An app that would provide a multitude of resources specifically related to completing one's work, located all in one place; functionality might include MLA, APA, or other formatting styles; a math problem solver; a dictionary and thesaurus; language translators; search; timelines and time management devices; and so on
- A status update for study groups
- A repository for sample papers

Student Survey

After the design workshop was completed, the Winter 2010 Student Mobile Devices and Website Survey (centered on tech ownership/use and web use) was created in SurveyMonkey and administered via iPad to 38 undergrad and grad students approached at random in the library. We basically walked around and asked students if they would be willing to take a five minute survey and offered them some snacks. This gave us the opportunity to engage in informal, personal conversation with the students while they took the survey. Although we did not collect date from these informal chats, we did determine that if relevant data was uncovered during the conversations we could begin carrying around a sound recorder. Students reacted very positively to the survey being on an iPad. At the time of the survey, the idea of using an iPad for data collection was relatively cutting edge. The first generation iPad had been released only six months prior and many students had not yet had the opportunity to use one at that point. We received comments from students telling us "how cool" it was that the library owned one of these devices and were using it in this manner. We speculated that students seemed more eager to take our survey for the chance to use and talk about the iPad.

During the course of our research, our sub-team also consulted the Spring 2010 and Spring 2012 student surveys conducted by University of Rochester IT. In its 2010 report, the survey's parameters are described: "In February and March 2010, approximately 4,509 University of Rochester students were asked to complete a survey regarding their experience and attitudes with information technology at the institution. The survey consisted of 25 multiple-choice questions that utilize a Likert-type scale and two open ended questions to assess their experience with IT. The web-based survey was conducted from February 23–March 8 with a 36% return rate—1,637 undergraduate responses." The 2012 study was conducted within similar parameters. Utilizing the existing data compiled in these studies allowed us to spend more time interpreting the data, identifying areas where we wanted to collect additional data, and brainstorming ideas for developing new offerings.

Findings

The information we gathered confirmed what we expected: Students own numerous technology devices and use them heavily throughout the day, and faculty members are also heavy users of computers, laptops, phones, and so on.

The majority of the students we interviewed own at least a laptop and laptop use far exceeds desktop use. Most students also own a cell phone, and SMS messaging is ubiquitous. Numerous students own an Internet-capable mobile device, whether a smart phone, iPod, or other device, and these numbers are growing steadily. However, many students reported finding the pricing of data plans prohibitive, opting in some cases to use smart phones only for regular calling and texting.

Social media continue to be very important to students, the majority focusing their use on only a few major websites and applications. Students currently use mobile devices—other than laptops and netbooks—for primarily so-cial, rather than academic, purposes. However, many with whom we spoke directly about the matter were open to the latter idea. The design workshop we co-conducted may be instructive in this regard. As noted, the main activity of the workshop involved the participants designing either a mobile app that would support anything having to do with study groups or an app that would support anything having to do with writing a research paper. All participants chose to develop an app that supported study groups. There are a couple of possible reasons for this. First, students may already employ tried-and-true methods when undertaking research. An app supporting research might be seen as disruptive to these methods, simply adding more busy work to an already complex set of tasks. Second, apps may be seen as primarily social. Study groups are a social activity, whereas writing a research paper is more of a singular task. Do students view emerging technology as primarily social in nature?

Regarding student use of technology in academic work, nearly all students believe that technology or the web enhances their learning. They want easier access to reliable information for their work from anywhere and from any device. Students frequently collaborate on academic projects and are looking for ways to do so more efficiently. A majority of students are currently satisfied with technology at the University of Rochester, though they sometimes express needs for services the library already offers. Significantly, according to University IT's student surveys, students view wireless networking as a basic utility service and feel strongly that it should be available all over campus.

Most of the few faculty members we interviewed require students to use e-mail, the Internet, and Blackboard for their coursework. Our interviews indicated that faculty ownership of laptops, cell phones, and smart phones appears to be on par with that of students, though the level of faculty engagement with technology varies widely.

Moving Forward

How can we use this information about student and faculty use of applications and devices to enhance the student learning experience?

With technology and digital offerings, we must move quickly on development and deployment to stay relevant, let alone on the cutting edge. A challenge to the sub-team's work has been how quickly technology changes. Some of our findings and methods could already be considered old and out of date. But several ideas for services and technology implementations occurred to us.

We can do more to promote technological resources that are already available—especially free online resources and apps and those offered by the University of Rochester and River Campus Libraries—to meet students' academic and social needs. We, as a library, should continue to offer services and resources specifically designed for mobile devices and be nimble and innovative in developing such new tools as the library's mobile site and our "Text me this call number" service.

We want to produce and display content in creative ways that will enhance consumption of the content and the learning that stems from it. We could provide students with a personalized list of resources and links based on a web-based survey page. We could feature an app or database of the month on the River Campus Libraries' website to highlight underutilized resources. An online suggestion box for the purpose of continually collecting new ideas from students, faculty, and staff regarding new online and mobile tools could be very helpful. Ultimately, regular, active, systematic communication with students is essential for monitoring emerging technological trends and evolving needs. Towards the same end, we might observe the activities of progressive academic libraries on these fronts. It will be essential, we think, to mainstream support for mobile and SMS-based services, putting them on par with other digital offerings.

Additionally, while we confined ourselves to gathering information on the technology use of our students and faculty, it might also prove worthwhile to examine the technology experience of River Campus Libraries staff members. We wonder whether it might be helpful to develop an individualized "text-a-librarian" service for each subject librarian or explore opportunities to provide or develop a service that will enable university members to connect with each other for collaborative research and study opportunities, providing an academic social networking tool of sorts. Many more such ideas could be developed.

Perhaps most importantly, it seems safe to assume that the number of undergrads using laptops/netbooks and Internet-enabled handheld devices, such as smart phones and iPads, will continue to grow rapidly. Our university and library system should always have this in mind when exploring or developing new technologies and services. As mentioned above, the survey we administered via iPad elicited several positive comments from the participants regarding the library's use of new technology. This strategy also allowed us to interact in a personal way with students even though the information we were gathering was quantitative and could have been easily obtained without any actual person-to-person contact. It may be that skillful use of up-to-date technical resources by library staff will be key in fostering the perception among students of the library as an ever-relevant, evolving support for their academic work.

Notes

1. The Applications and Devices sub-team comprised Solomon Blaylock and Cynthia Carlton (co-leaders) along with Ann Marshall and Nathan Sarr.

2. We conducted a design workshop in cooperation with the Design Workshop sub-team.

chapter four. **Picture My Work**

Judi Briden and Sarada George

The visual sociologist Douglas Harper uses photographs to elicit extensive information about the lives of others (see, for example, Harper, 1982, 1986, and 2002). Inspired by his work, a team at the University of Rochester's River Campus Libraries asked undergraduate students to take photographs of their research tools, communication devices, favorite places to do their work, and even their favorite shoes. When we interviewed students about their photos, they provided thorough and detailed information about their academic work and how it fits into their lives. In this chapter, we give a brief description of our method and then share what we learned from analyzing student photos and interview transcripts. We argue that the photo elicitation method, though quick and easy, provides compelling information and important insights into the lives and the work of our students.

The Rochester Studies

In 2004–2005, we first conducted photo elicitation interviews with eight undergraduates, as described in Chapter 5 of *Studying Students: The Undergraduate Research Project at the University of Rochester* (Briden, 2007, pp. 40–47). Other libraries, drawing on our work, have conducted their own photo elicitation interviews. Published studies include the multi-institutional ERIAL Project led by Northeastern Illinois University, a study at Fresno State, the MIT Photo Diary Study, and a space study at Edmonton Public Library (see Appendix 4A).

Six years after our original research, we wondered how much might have changed and whether, in repeating the photo elicitation study, we would gain new insights or at least update our findings. Our 2011 study involved 10 students. As in the first study, we gave students a list of photographs we wanted them to take of the places and objects they interact with on a daily basis. Each student was then interviewed individually and had the opportunity to describe the photos while viewing them and to answer questions about them.

For our original research in 2004–2005, we prepared a list of 20 photographs that we asked students to take. In 2011, we used a slightly different list of 22 items (see Appendix 4B). Fourteen of the photo requests remained substantially unchanged for the two studies, including "all the stuff you take to class," "your communication devices," and "a picture of your room, showing your computer." We made some changes for the second study in order to focus more on library and campus spaces and to elicit student perceptions about those spaces. We wanted to have a more granular understanding of the spaces students choose for particular activities and why. To this end, we asked students to photograph three kinds of "great places:" to do homework, to study for a test or quiz, and to work on a paper. Then, we asked them to show us "another great place" for each of these same three activities. From the original photo list, we also eliminated questions that asked students to photograph others as privacy considerations took precedence; we specifically instructed our participants in the second study not to include identifiable people in their photographs. Finally, we dropped a few questions that were relatively unproductive and substituted others. For example, we dropped the question asking students to photograph something they thought others did not know about, but added the item about showing your favorite pair of shoes. Although a favorite pair of shoes may not seem relevant to what we wanted to learn, it is an important reminder to the researchers that students have full lives beyond the purposes of our interviews and deserve our complete respect. The students we interviewed are much more than the sum of those parts that we examined, and we sincerely thank them for their participation.

In the spring of 2011, after revising the list of photographs we would ask students to take, we recruited four freshmen, two sophomores, and four seniors to take photographs showing various aspects of their lives on campus. When each student returned with the photos taken using a digital camera, he or she was individually interviewed about what appeared in the photographs and also asked iterative questions that surfaced while viewing the images. Interviews were audio recorded and transcribed. Not every student took photographs of everything on the list, so for some questions the number of responses was lower than would be expected. The images and transcripts in combination constitute an in-depth investigation into specific aspects of that student's preferences, experiences, and strategies as an undergraduate at the University of Rochester.

Picturing Spaces

In both of our studies, six years apart, students expressed the need for different kinds of spaces for engaging in different academic activities. In the aggregate, these needs exhibited the same contrast and pull between opposites—quiet, comfortably busy; some distractions, no distractions; with friends, alone; in the library, in the dorm; open and bright, enclosed and focused;

working, relaxing; surrounded by books, sitting by windows. It seems that students need a variety of spaces in which to work, including some that will allow them to escape from the constant connection to electronic devices.

Comparing the older and newer interviews, some elements stood out. In 2011, a higher proportion of students preferred to do academic work in library spaces rather than in dorms or other campus locations. Although some students still expressed a preference for working in their dorms for specific activities, many identified areas in the library that they felt were best suited to accomplishing their academic tasks. In answering our three "great places" questions (for doing homework, studying for a test or quiz, and working on a paper), students photographed library spaces 36 times, dorm spaces 12 times, and other campus locations six times. The locations most often referenced were library stacks, the Gleason Library, and the Messinger Periodical Reading Room (PRR). The library stacks offer quiet, less-frequented spaces with carrels and small tables as well as spaces with larger tables that can accommodate groups. The Gleason Library is the most popular study space on campus with a variety of seating, plenty of natural light, nearby food, and constant traffic into and out of the area. The Messinger Periodical Reading Room is a large traditional library space with high ceilings and windows, journals on perimeter shelving, heavy wooden tables, and a very quiet atmosphere enforced by the users.

An interesting difference between freshman and senior responses in 2011 was that no freshman named the Messinger Periodical Reading Room (PRR), which is usually drop-dead quiet, as a great place for any of the academic activities we asked about. Similarly, no senior named the Gleason Library, usually free-flowing and somewhat noisy, as a great place for any of these same activities. Additionally, freshmen named dorm locations as great places more often than seniors.

Table 4.1. Great Places to Do Academic Work, 2011			
Great Places	**4 Freshmen**	**2 Sophomores**	**4 Seniors**
To do homework			
Library spaces			
Gleason	2		
PRR			2
Stacks		1	3
Other in library		2	
Total in library	**2**	**3**	**5**
Dorm spaces	3		2
Other campus spaces	1	1	1
To study for a test or quiz			
Library spaces			
Gleason	4		
PRR		2	2
Stacks			1
Other in library		2	3
Total in library	**4**	**4**	**6**
Dorm spaces	2		
Other campus spaces			2
To work on a paper			
Library spaces			
Gleason		1	
PRR			1
Stacks	2	2	2
Other in library	1		3
Total in library	**3**	**3**	**6**
Dorm spaces	3		2
Other campus spaces		1	
Totals for all 3 academic activities			
Library spaces			
Gleason	6	1	
PRR		2	5
Stacks	2	3	6
Other in library	1	4	6
Total in library	**9**	**10**	**17**
Dorm spaces	8		4
Other campus spaces	1	2	3
Totals for all spaces	**18**	**12**	**24**

That freshmen, who are relatively new to campus, feel comfortable doing academic work in the dorms is hardly surprising; dorms are spaces where they have spent the most time since coming to college and these spaces "belong" to them. Among library spaces, the Gleason Library is a prime location for group activities, open 24 hours a day, and freshmen are heavy users of this space. So, freshman preferences for doing academic work in their dorms and Gleason Library seem reasonable. Seniors, presumably, are more familiar with many areas on campus, and over time have identified locations that work for what they want to do in any particular instance. Perhaps students change their choices of suitable spaces as they progress in their college careers. If so, does this reflect changing criteria or simply wider knowledge of the available options? Another possibility is that the qualities of a particular space may change based on the expectations of those who are using it, and the population of users changes over time. Further research might help answer these questions.

Related perhaps to increased preferences for library spaces, there were significantly more mentions by all students in the 2011 interviews of the words "quiet," "silence," and "focus" than in 2004–2005. This may indicate that students are finding it more important, or that it is becoming more difficult, to locate suitable conditions for concentrating on academic work and that the library more often supplies the right conditions.

Well, I think it's just a combination of factors. Definitely the quietness is nice. Everybody is focused on work. If you're there, you're there to get work done.

When I work on a paper, I like to work in a very silent area. As you can see, it's a cubicle with not a lot of interaction with anybody.

In the latest interviews, we also identified differences in the way freshmen and seniors talked about suitable spaces for doing academic work. Freshmen are still discovering what spaces work for them as they undertake different activities. They are trying to figure out the characteristics of spaces and what is a good match for what they want to do. Finding spaces that are available when they want to use them is also an issue.

So I sit there by myself and bend over a table and do homework, and I am quiet because it's the quieter room, but it really bothers me that people go in and out, and they're loud." —Freshman talking about the "quieter" area in Gleason Library

That is my bed. It's a great place to do homework. I have my room set up so that the head of my bed is behind my wardrobe, so I can actually hide behind it. When you walk in, you can't see me because I'll be hidden behind my wardrobe. So I can just camp out in my bed, get all my books, the answer books, all my notebooks, and my calculator, and just turn on a light, sit up against my pillows, and just lie back. And nobody can really—people can see my legs when they walk in, but I'm isolated by my wardrobe, so it's not as distracting. —Freshman talking about doing homework in her dorm room

Figure 4.1. One student's great place to do homework: her dorm room

I personally like working on tables, but my friends don't, so sometimes we just end up gathering a couple of those chairs….But usually we're by the windows and not at the tables because a lot of times the tables are taken. —Freshman talking about Gleason Library

I usually do my homework and stuff, just wherever there's an open seat in Gleason. — Freshman talking about Gleason Library

More often, seniors have learned what spaces work for them and what qualities are important. They have identified the best places for what they specifically want to do and are comfortable using them.

When I'm writing a paper, I like it to be really quiet. I don't tend to listen to music when I'm doing it. And I like there to be a hard surface like a table; it's better than working in a chair. So PRR's perfect. —Senior talking about the Messinger Periodical Reading Room as a great place to work on a paper

I like the fact that it's near a window because you can open it up if you get too hot and just get a little fresh air. I got the outlet in the picture there. That's really important because I need to be able to plug in my laptop, and then also on Level 300 you can still get the Internet. That works well. —Senior talking about a great place in the library stacks to study for a test or quiz

This is the fourth floor of Wilson Commons— another bridge lounge. And it tends to be pretty quiet up here, and not too many people go, and then it's also very open, so I like that about it. —Senior talking about a great place in the student commons to study for a test or quiz

The scholarly atmosphere of the library was another important element for students. Several

Figure 4.2. A senior's great place in the stacks to study for a test or quiz

told us that the library was a place to do academic work and they counted on that quality to keep them on task.

I like the sort of old aesthetic of wood and books and things around me when I'm studying.

I think the fact that it's a library makes me feel like I should be getting my work done.

I believe that in the library you have access to a lot of books, and even though a lot of my research encompasses papers that are published on the Internet and I access that from anywhere, being in the library kind of puts me in the mindset of having to do some scientific research. And if I do need a book, I can always look on the catalog and take out a book or a journal from one of the places in the library.

Figure 4.3. Bridge lounge in Wilson Commons: one student's great place to study for a test or quiz

Even though students were clear about the qualities of a particular space, their assessments did not necessarily agree with each other. Students' attitudes about two popular spaces in Rush Rhees Library revealed contrasting views on how well they worked for any particular individual.

Messinger Periodical Reading Room (PRR)
- Absolutely quiet, so you can get work done
- It's okay to talk quietly
- People moving around are distracting
- Good tables for working alone
- Others glare if you make any noise
- Pretentious, no one is working that hard

Gleason Library
- Disorganized free-for-all, messy
- Social space for relaxing
- Good for collaborating with others
- Good for mixing work and breaks
- Too loud and noisy to focus
- It's okay to be loud because others are loud

Whether students embrace or decry the qualities of a specific space, they must have access to an assortment of spaces that will support the varied tasks and purposes they have at any particular time. From the student's perspective, the goal is to have at least one good space available that is suited to whatever it is he or she needs to do now. Doing homework, studying for a test or quiz, working on a paper—in students' eyes, these have different space requirements. Of the 10 students interviewed in 2011, only four named the same location for more than one of these tasks. In the aggregate, they named 21 different locations, 14 of them in the library. From the library's perspective, having well-used spaces is an indication that we are meeting specific needs of students at any particular time, and a variety of spaces with different qualities will always be required.

Another reason the students we interviewed chose to work in a particular space was the sub-

Figure 4.4. Messinger Periodical Reading Room

Figure 4.5. One section of the Gleason Library

ject being worked on; they told us about qualities needed to accomplish work in certain subjects.

I feel like linguistics I could pretty much do anywhere, just because it's a lot less intense. It's also more writing based, so like I said I work in Starbucks or somewhere that's a little bit more distracting. Engineering I like to have it really quiet.

Well, it depends what kind of work I'm doing. If I'm working on a paper, then I only need a computer, which fits perfectly on the little table. But if I'm doing German homework, which requires my textbook, my workbook, my notes, and maybe a computer, then I'd want to spread out and not be confined to the table in my lap.

Feeling Lost

We asked students in 2011 to photograph a place *in the library* that they avoided or where they felt lost. (The similar question in 2004–2005 had referred only to feeling lost.) A lower percentage

Figure 4.6. Chairs with lap tables are fine for some kinds of work, but not for other kinds

of students named the library stacks in 2011: 40%, compared to 57% in 2004–2005. Forty percent is still not ideal, but it is at least trending in the right direction. This may be the result of efforts that the library made between the two studies to improve way-finding and access to the collections. Or it may simply reflect increased use of the stacks as study spaces and reduced pressure to locate physical materials. It was interesting to see that four students in 2011, compared to only one in 2004–2005, took photographs of places in the library where they had never been before. After interviewing them, we interpreted this to mean that they felt comfortable in the library spaces that they had used and simply went somewhere they had not been before to take the requested photo.

In response to a similar question in 2011 about a place *on campus* that they avoided or where they felt lost, most of the photographs were of such outdoor locations as the outsides of buildings, open plazas, or walkways. Many showed open areas between buildings that the students did not frequent. Interestingly, two students independently used the word "barren" to describe the places they had photographed. Commenting on why they took the photographs they did, students expressed a feeling of strangeness or a feeling of not belonging in those spaces. Again, four of the responses showed a place where the student had never been before.

The idea that there are spaces in the library and on campus where students feel awkward or like interlopers is regrettable. Certainly, not all spaces can be open and welcoming, but very likely more of them can be than actually are. This is a problem that might be approached using a variety of strategies. Our goal should be to make all areas of the university libraries welcoming and inviting, rather than intimidating. We have been working on this for a number of years and will continue to do so.

The libraries' Scare Fair, held at Halloween, is one such activity. While enjoying costumes, entertainment, and snacks in the library, students are encouraged to explore the stacks to find specific books and are rewarded with a tour of the Rush Rhees Tower on top of the library. Students flock to this event every year, learning a bit more about navigating the stacks and increasing their familiarity with library spaces in the process.

Another strategy to help students become familiar with different areas of the River Campus Libraries was a "Bucket List." Developed by library assistant Mari Tsuchiya in 2012, the poster suggests 23 fun and interesting activities for students to try before they graduate. Activities include eating lunch on the library balcony, finding your favorite study spot, impressing your professor with a source from Rare Books and Special Collections, checking out a movie from the Multimedia Center, and seeing the first photocopier in Carlson Library. We handed out the poster and bookmarks at the Technology Expo held during freshman orientation. Such a list may spark incoming students' awareness of and curiosity about the library, and we hope it will be used in future orientations.[1]

Studying with Friends

As we try to make students feel more comfortable in the library, one of the most important considerations is the way they use library spaces in association with other people. The question of studying alone or with others came up in many of our interviews and, although we discouraged photos of people in 2011, it is clear that studying is not necessarily a solitary activity and it seems to have become less solitary over time. Students frequently study with or near other people.

There were almost twice as many references to friends in our 2011 photo interviews as there were six years earlier. This does not necessarily mean that students had more friends the second time, but there is a possibility that they were spending more time doing academic work with

them. Students indicated that they would study in a space selected by friends even when the space itself was not otherwise desirable to them.

This is one of the Gleason studios, where I sometimes study. My friends like to go there, so I go with them. It's got nice big tables, and you're sort of walled off from the rest of them.

Generally I'm in the Great Hall if I'm in the library because that's where my friends are clustered, and they don't like how hot the PRR can get at times. I'm the opposite—I love warmth; I'm cold all the time, so I would prefer to be in the PRR usually.

More students also mentioned studying in groups rather than studying alone or with a single study partner. In the first photo elicitation study, four people mentioned studying with a roommate or a single "study buddy" from a class they were taking. In the second study, only one person mentioned studying with a single partner, and, in that case, the professor had encouraged the practice. More than two people were involved in other mentions of group studying.

It is important to make a distinction between organized study groups and informal situations where a number of friends are studying together.[2] Organized study groups are more often composed of people from the same class who arrange to meet, usually on a regular basis, to deal with either specific assignments or general work in the class they are all taking. Other groupings are less formal, less scheduled, and often involve students taking completely different courses. The phenomenon of friends studying together covers a range of fluid and informal activity, from suitemates who happen to be working in the suite lounge at the same time to a group of friends going to a selected campus location to keep each other company and take breaks together. Referring to a dormitory lounge, one student informed us that "it's right down the hall from my room and half of my friends live on my hall, so the other half of my friends join and we just all sit there and do homework." Friends studying together may interact on course material, whether from the same or different courses. For example, students preparing for exams may quiz each other on their separate subjects.

Working together on current assignments or studying for exams may be easier to do now, when more students carry their laptops around, than earlier, when many of them were constrained to find a place that already had computers. One student noted, "I have a big group of friends and generally we all sit around with our laptops." The result may be a great many computers in the same place, something much easier to arrange with laptops than with desktop computers. Institutional computer clusters are no longer the only place for students to work together with computers. In fact, such clusters might now be considered much less convenient for working alongside friends.

It might seem that studying together in a group would interfere with getting work done, but students do not seem to feel that this happens in these informal groups. They believe that working with friends actually discourages them from succumbing to the ever-present distractions on their laptops, with the promise of spending some leisure time together when the work is finished or paused:

That helps me stay focused; I'm not as likely to go online or check something else…. I know they are working just as hard and I want to like finish at the same time so we can go do something fun. More motivational.

Keeping each other on task is a real benefit of working together, but some students feel that friends can provide even more direct assistance with homework or studying:

A lot of it conceptually is difficult, so it helps me a lot if I work with my friends. I have friends who are in the same classes—there's one friend in particular. I help him with chemistry and he helps me with physics, so it's a really good partnership.

This desire of friends to help each other could be useful from a library point of view. A student needing assistance with library resources might be more willing to ask another student who works at the library than to approach a librarian at the desk. One student mentioned this specifically:

And a lot of my friends, they work at the library, so they'll be at the desk and I'll just sit right there and write my paper, or something … I am more likely to ask them for help than if I didn't know the person behind the desk.

For many students, studying in proximity to friends boosts concentration. As one student put it, "I think with other people around, doing the same work that I'm doing, I'm more focused on my work." But not everyone wants to have others around. Several students said they were unable to study with friends nearby. As one said, "I can't really work with my friends around." And several said they needed silence to study for exams. But there are many ways to work with or without others. One student who did not want to work with friends liked to have some people around to ask for help if necessary, even though they were not actually studying together.

While there is evidence that studying together has positive effects on learning, some researchers question its efficacy. Richard Arum and Josipa Roksa, in their book *Academically Adrift: Limited Learning on College Campuses* (2011), find that collaborative studying has either no effect or a negative effect on student learning. They do mention, however, that their data may be affected by improper use of collaborative learning, that students may not be sufficiently focused on their studies when working with others (Arum & Roksa, 2011, Chapter 5). They also recognize that the effects of collaborative learning may vary across academic fields, writing, "Moreover, collaborative learning strategies have been promoted heavily by the National Science Foundation and others in the science fields. It is possible that in those fields, which tend to have structured assignments and exams, study groups outside of class are advantageous" (Arum & Roksa, 2011, p. 102). The authors urge that more information be obtained before universities rush fully to embrace the group study model:

> We are not questioning the possibility of students having enlightening theoretical discussions outside of the classroom and learning from their peers, but our results caution against the overarching emphasis on peer studying, until we know more about how and under what conditions those experiences occur and are able to enhance student learning (Arum & Roksa, 2011, p. 102).

Students studying together can be working in proximity to each other rather than collaborating. Friends may be important in the intervals rather than for studying itself. After a period of intensive work, a break is welcome. As one student said, "I can't just sit down and work on homework for about four hours."

Students place themselves in relation to other people according to their needs at the time and follow local convention and an informal "space etiquette" that has developed around the use of various library locations. Certain rooms are understood to be quiet study areas where individuals work alone and students are careful not to sit too close to someone else except when the entire room is becoming full. The first person

to sit at a table is considered to have a claim to the whole table, until the room starts to fill up:

> I guess I feel like you have a "right" to the whole table if there is another place for people to sit, but if there isn't, then it's acceptable to share. It's kind of like how close you would sit to somebody in a train station. You would never sit down in the seat right next to somebody unless it was the only seat.

> Generally, I feel like it's socially acceptable to share a table if there is just one person there and there's no place else open. And it's also definitely easier if you are just one person yourself. So if I was with a friend, we would hesitate to sit at a table with one person, but if the library was really full, like during finals week, we would definitely do it.

By these unwritten rules, two students who want to work next to each other without much interaction may use an area where individuals are working alone, but a group of people who intend to collaborate would have to look for larger tables where noise was acceptable. Others could then come by and join the group. One student remarked about a group at a table, "Actually, the whole table was filled with people I knew."

Keeping in Touch

Within the lifetimes of our recent students, communication among students on campus and between students and their friends and relatives outside the University has become easier to accomplish and more difficult to escape. Whether they are studying together or not, students have plenty of opportunity to stay in touch with their friends. Cell phones have become ubiquitous and a major means of communication. When asked to photograph their communication tools and what they carry around with them regularly, every student in the 2011 group included a cell phone as did nearly everyone in the 2004–2005 group. Some used their phones as alarm clocks and watches. Some used them for e-mail. Nearly all used their phones primarily, or to a great extent, for texting and not as much for voice calling.

Most voice calling was reserved for out-of-town family and friends. Texting was the method of choice for communication on campus, so as not to disturb friends during classes or because it was faster for arranging to meet. One student mentioned the advantages of asynchronous communication by texting:

> One of the things is that you get to answer a text at any time of the day. However, when you get a phone call, you kind of feel obligated to pick up or call somebody back if you miss.

Landline telephones seem to have gone out of use altogether. Even in our earlier photos, where one or two landline phones are evident, students hardly ever used them. By 2011, not one landline showed up in a photograph. But there is a great deal of variation in student communica-

Figure 4.7. Every student interviewed used a cell phone

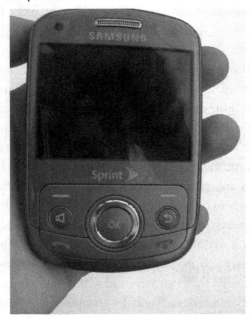

tion. The student above who liked to answer texts when convenient also mentioned calling friends frequently, but they "get bothered by it because they're in class when I'm calling them. They say, 'Text me instead.'" Though all students seemed to have cell phones, they were not all "smart" in 2011, in spite of advances in technology. Several took photos of flip phones or other earlier types with fewer capabilities, though none mentioned lacking texting capability.

Some students used e-mail often and others did not. They e-mailed from their phones, their laptops, or campus computers. Some who did not e-mail or use the Internet from their cell phones cited expense as the reason for avoiding it. Regardless of how they accessed it, students saw e-mail as more formal than texting. Several said they e-mailed professors, and one mentioned e-mailing fellow board members of campus clubs. Others still said they used e-mail for everything. It is difficult to tell whether or how much this has changed since the earlier interviews, but there seems to be more variability between students than between the two sets of interviews.

Some of the communication differences we noticed may be due to changes in the focus of follow-up questions between the two sets of interviews. Even though the basic questions were the same, we followed a slightly different approach in subsequent questions. For example, in follow-up questions in the first set of interviews we asked more about social media like Facebook and MySpace, while in the second set we asked more about cell phone use and laptops. In 2011, the interviewer did not ask explicitly about use of social media.

In 2004–2005, our interviewees frequently spoke about instant messaging (IM). IM appears much less frequently in 2011, but Skype, Google chat, Facebook chat, and similar communication methods were mentioned. At least two of the earlier students specifically noted that electronic communication and gadgetry were isolating;

they preferred face-to-face interactions. We noticed no such comments in 2011, but students did make clear choices about technology, using older or newer types for different purposes. Several students even wrote physical letters with pen and paper. "Stationery," said one, "I write letters to my friends and my friends write letters back." Mixed use of older and newer technologies is one of the most notable of our findings.

Choosing Technologies

Most students coming to the library today bring their own laptops. Laptops were mentioned in every interview and appeared in many of the photos as items that are carried around in their backpacks. When students mentioned using a library computer, it was generally because they had access to free printing in a department or area where they were employed. Easily portable computers and other electronic communication devices have clearly become ubiquitous, making finding fixed computers less necessary.

Not only do students use their laptops to write their papers, they use them increasingly for both work and play. This can lead to distraction. As some students noted, it can be difficult to avoid social networking when it is available on the same device you are using to write your paper. And although students are definitely using high technology devices in their daily lives, there does not appear to be a headlong rush into a high-tech, paperless world. They are making choices about what technology to use when and for what reason, and sometimes even whether to use technology at all.

In nearly everything our students do, from scheduling their time to writing their papers, they have to make choices of how and when to use technology. In both studies, a surprising number of students used low-tech scheduling aids to manage their time. Nearly half of the students in the 2011 group still used a physical planner or agenda book, though more of them used an electronic

scheduler than in 2004–2005. Two mentioned Google Calendar and one used iCal, either in addition to or instead of paper methods. Fewer relied solely on their memories, though. Almost every student used some kind of scheduling aid to keep track of classes, assignments, and appointments, whether it was a paper pocket calendar or an iPhone. Some even used sticky notes left around in their dorm rooms, on their notebooks, or electronic post-it notes on their computers.

Figure 4.8. Low-tech paper schedulers were used as often as electronic ones

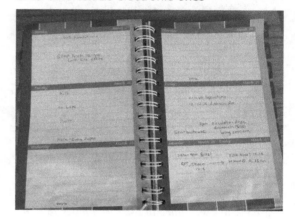

This use of a range of high and low technologies was particularly noticeable when students talked about writing or preparing to write their papers. They all had computers and all used them, but paper and pen or pencil were evident everywhere, in combination with all the advanced technology.

Our earlier study had found three students using index cards to take notes while researching papers. Cards were not mentioned in 2011, but it was evident that writing tools were chosen carefully. Some read articles on their computers but more used computers mostly for writing. At least one reported computerizing the entire paper process. Others said they found computers distracting when working. They tended to know exactly why they did or did not use technology for a particular task.

Figure 4.9. For writing tasks, paper and newer technologies were both used

Everyone types on computer now. Everything's typed on computer. But for research papers, every step I use the computer. Even if I'm going to find a book to use, I have to use a computer to find that book.

I don't take notes on computers. That doesn't work for me and then I'll get distracted, since I'll have Internet with me right there. So I hand write everything I do.

It is clear that student use of technology for academics was highly personal; it may vary depending on who will see the finished product as well as on their idiosyncratic processes:

In my writing class, if I were to write an essay, I'd have to use my laptop because you have to pass it in … if I'm doing homework or filling something out, I always use a pencil and paper.

So I normally take a lot of notes in a notebook and then work on an outline, and then while I'm doing

that, I'll start writing paragraphs that just pop into my mind. But I don't generally start writing the paper itself until I have many pages of written notes. And then when I start actually writing the paper, it's electronically in a Word document.

We saw a similar reliance on both older and newer technology in reading. Our earlier study found many students printing out articles to read for papers. This time, one student specifically mentioned that she refrained from printing articles she found online, though she used information from physical books:

This last paper, I kept all of the PDF's on my computer because they were all like 100 pages, and I didn't want to print them out. But you would see the research books with the other sources laying around with papers sticking out of them.

The multiplicity of electronic devices available to today's students allows them to customize their interaction with the world both academically and socially and to alternate between the two quite easily. With headphones, earbuds, smart phones, laptops, tablets, MP3 players, and the campus wireless network, students can work or socialize in almost any location on campus. We must assume that other factors come into play when they choose to work in the library since they can easily access the world of electronic information on their own or on public devices in many other campus locations.

Blending Print and Digital

Though digital books are available, many students still make use of physical, printed books and textbooks. But while books and other printed materials showed up in 2011 photos of dorm rooms and backpacks, we saw many fewer than in the photos in 2004–2005. Combined with information we have gathered from other sources, we conclude that students now are using these printed materials less than before.

Some of this decrease may be due to the rapidly increasing cost of printed textbooks. Students are reluctant to purchase course texts, especially if they are expensive or if they are not convinced that the professor will actually require the use of the text. On the latter point, one student told us, "Well, actually, I don't really use my books, so … Like, they ask you to get books but you never use them." The library puts many textbooks on reserve and provides electronic access to increasing amounts of course material, so the information in textbooks is often freely available and does not require that a student purchase an expensive book.

In addition to assigned course reading, students took photographs of books they have for leisure reading. Even very busy students seemed to plan for this and called our interviewer's attention to their non-academic books. When asked to take pictures of their books, they often made a distinction between course books and those they had brought from home or acquired here for recreational reading, keeping them in different places or on different sides of a shelf. Whether there were few books or many, some were chosen for students' enjoyment, and they tended to be physical books. We did not see photos of Kindles or other electronic readers, though students may own them or read books online on their phones, laptops, or tablets for recreation.

The most-photographed type of book in this study was not an ordinary book, but a notebook. Though some students took notes on laptops, a surprising number carried multiple notebooks around with them and used them daily. They still seemed to use notebooks frequently for class notes, exam preparation, projects, homework, and notes for papers.

There was wide variation in what and how many items students carried around in their backpacks. Some, especially those living off campus or far from the location of most of their classes, did not plan to go home until evening and thus carried everything they would need for the day. When going to classes, they usually had

Figure 4.10. There were fewer textbooks in photographs and more personal books

notebooks, pens, pencils, their cell phones, and laptops, in addition to some personal items. In contrast, the subset of things they always carried everywhere might be minimal, including only a phone, ID, and perhaps keys. This did not seem to have changed between our two photo studies; in both, the cell phone did not seem to be optional.

In analyzing the interviews, we have begun to ask new questions. Students are using their laptops and other portable devices more and more for entertainment and social activities in addition to academic work. What is the impact of having mixed-use devices almost always present when doing academic work? Only one student we interviewed told us how she tried to eliminate distractions from technology.

> *I think the fact that it's a library makes me feel like I should be getting my work done, and there's nothing to distract me. I don't bring a computer, I try to turn my phone off if I'm in the library, just so I can only do the work that I brought.*

Figure 4.11. Notebooks were the most common type of books in photographs

Figure 4.12. What students take to class and what they always carry

The other students we interviewed all mentioned having their computers with them when they were working in library spaces. We hope in future interviews to learn more about students' efforts to balance work and relaxation with mixed-use devices.

Students Want Choices

Students enjoy wide latitude in doing their work their way, that is, in the way that enables them to use their strengths and take advantage of their academic opportunities. In photos and interviews, we see students customize everything from the way they do their work to how they socialize, all the while making use of multiple devices, tools, and processes. Students realize that they do not have to do things in the same way as their friends, even when they are doing the same things together. Is working alongside friends easier when it is possible to filter out distractions, mask ambient noise, and yet still take breaks together to watch YouTube? Is working alongside friends more desirable as a way to counteract the isolation of using technology to customize and filter what you pay attention to? Perhaps this was a factor in the higher number of references to friends in our 2011 interviews. An increase in mobile technology allows students to make these choices to stay in contact with their friends whether or not they are in physical proximity to them. It is easier now to satisfy both social and academic needs at the same time.

Comparing the photo elicitation interviews of 2011 to those of 2004–2005, we see that library spaces have increased as preferred study areas for students, that studying with friends is becoming more important, and that, at the same time, students are concerned with atmosphere, noise, and their ability to focus. While students are happy to use technology in a variety of ways to maintain connections to friends, they also express the need at times to be electronically unavailable; they need places to which they can retreat and, perhaps, disconnect.

As devices and applications permeate student life more and more, we will surely see further change in what students do and what they value in the library. And while this change is inevitable, it is not very predictable. However, while it is impossible to tell how our circumstances will change over the next five or 10 years, there are some predictions we can make and some preemptive actions we must assuredly take.

As students adapt their work and play to the sort of technology discussed above and as technology continues to develop, libraries must adapt continuously as well. The proliferation of devices and the way they make student work and play

independent of place requires that libraries, first of all, make all library data and functions readily usable on mobile devices and provide a wide range of library spaces for working and studying. Libraries must also provide knowledgeable technical assistance in using all library resources, developing new forms of face-to-face interaction with library staff to do so. We have begun to make some parts of our libraries' websites usable on mobile devices, but we believe that we will soon have to redevelop our entire site for mobile use.

We plan to provide both collaborative and individual workspace in future renovations to our university's libraries as we have over the past several years. Future spaces will likely include labs to introduce students and faculty members to new technology and to promote future technological innovation.

When we plan spaces for future students, we should consider not only whether students are working together or alone and the range of auditory environments they prefer, but also the degree of technology students will be using. While more devices will become available and some spaces will be dedicated to learning to use them and "playing" with even newer devices, there will still be a need for escape from technology. The library must also provide spaces where students can "hide out" and be electronically unavailable while they work.

Student needs, technology, and libraries are all changing and will continue to do so at a rapid pace. In this context, we must continue to do research such as photo elicitation studies to keep ourselves focused on our patrons' needs and make sure we evolve in the same direction. Above all, if we want our libraries to remain relevant to students in the 21st century, we will have to find new ways to make ourselves accessible and responsive to our students and to include them in solving the problems they have helped us identify.

Appendix 4A. Published Photo-Elicitation Studies by Libraries

Briden, J. (2007). Photo surveys: Eliciting more than you knew to ask for. In N. F. Foster & S. Gibbons (Eds.), *Studying students: The undergraduate research project at the University of Rochester* (pp. 40–47). Chicago, IL: Association of College and Research Libraries.

Delcore, H.D., Mullolly, J., & Scroggins, M. (2009). *The library study at Fresno State.* Retrieved from http://www.fresnostate.edu/socialsciences/anthropology/ipa/thelibrarystudy.html

Duke, L.M. & Asher, A.D. (2011). *College libraries and student culture: What we now know.* Chicago, IL: ALA Editions.

Gabridge, T., Gaskell, M., & Stout, A. (2008). Information seeking through students' eyes: The MIT photo diary study. *College & Research Libraries, 69*(6), 510–522.

Haberl, V. & Wortman, B. (2012). Getting the picture: Interviews and photo elicitation at Edmonton Public Library. *LIBRES: Library and Information Science Research Electronic Journal, 22*(2), 1–21.

Keller, A. (2012). "In print or on screen? Investigating the reading habits of undergraduate students using photo-diaries and photo-interviews. *Libri, 62*(1), 1–18. doi:10.1515/libri-2012-0001

Lin, S. (2006). Perceptions of United States academic library services of first-year graduate students from Taiwan: A photo-elicitation study. (Doctoral dissertation). The University of Wisconsin–Madison. Retrieved from ProQuest Dissertations and Theses. (Order No. 3234607)

Appendix 4B. Photographs Requested for Photo Elicitation Studies

2011 List of Photos	2004–2005 List of Photos
The computer you use in the library, showing its surroundings	The computer you use in the library, showing its surroundings
All the stuff you take to class	All the stuff you take to class
Something that you would call "high tech"	Something that you would call "high tech"
Something really weird	Something really weird
The place you keep your books	The place you keep your books
Your communication devices	Your communication devices
A picture of your room, showing your computer	A picture of your dorm room, showing your computer
Another view of your room	Another view of your dorm room
How you schedule your time or keep track of your work	How you manage your time or keep track of your work
Your favorite part of the day	Your favorite part of the day
The tools you use for writing assignments	The tools you use for writing assignments
The things you always carry with you	The things you always carry with you
Something you can't live without	Something you can't live without
A place in the library that you avoid or where you feel lost	A place in the library where you feel lost
A place on campus that you avoid or where you feel lost	
A great place to do homework	
Another great place to do homework	
A great place to work on a paper	
Another great place to work on a paper	
A great place to study for a test or a quiz	
Another great place to study for a test or a quiz	
Your favorite shoes	
	The night before a big assignment is due
	Something you've noticed that you think others don't notice
	Your favorite person or people to study with
	A person, any person
	One picture of the libraries to show to a new freshman
	Your favorite place to study
	The rest: Whatever you want!

Notes

1. See the "Bucket List" poster PDF at http://docushare.lib.rochester.edu/docushare/dsweb/Get/Document-51166

2. See Chapter 10, "Study Groups in Libraries: Exponential Benefits," for a more extensive discussion of study groups.

References

Arum, R. & Roksa, J. (2011). *Academically adrift: Limited learning on college campuses.* Chicago, IL: University of Chicago Press.

Briden, J. (2007). Photo surveys: Eliciting more than you knew to ask for. In N. F. Foster & S. Gibbons (Eds.), *Studying students: The undergraduate research project at the University of Rochester* (pp. 40–47). Chicago, IL: Association of College and Research Libraries.

Harper, D.A. (1982). *Good company.* Chicago, IL: University of Chicago Press.

Harper, D.A. (1986). Meaning and work: A study in photo elicitation. *Current Sociology, 34*(3), 24–46. doi:10.1177/001139286034003006

Harper, D.A. (2002). "Talking about pictures: A case for photo elicitation. *Visual Studies, 17*(1), 13–26. doi:10.1080/14725860220137345

chapter five. **Learning the Ropes**

Marcy Strong, Kenn Harper, and Mari Tsuchiya

Over the last few years we have begun to gain a richer and deeper understanding of the lives of University of Rochester River Campus students. In our earlier study (Foster & Gibbons, 2007) we observed how the writing of term papers fit into our students' lives, extending into their relationships with their friends and parents, their employment, their social lives, and extra-curricular activities. After publishing our work in 2008, some of us became pre-major academic advisors and learned about the lives of our advisees in new ways; we became better acquainted with the significant changes that occur in their development as students and as young adults during their first two years of college, often before they declare a major. These experiences suggested that there was more to learn about how our undergraduates make the transition from high school seniors to college seniors, seen in our culture as a transition from childhood to adulthood (Arnett, 2004). For students, this is a time of learning more about their potential, experimenting, taking risks, and maturing into their fuller adult selves. Part of this process entails "learning the ropes"—figuring out how to make college work, becoming competent as students, identifying one's strengths and interests, and developing a body of experience and knowledge upon which to build an adult life.

To learn more about how students move through this transition at our university, we formed a team of librarians and library staff to conduct a series of interviews with academic advisors, resident advisors, and students.[1] We organized the interviews around specific moments in which students became knowledgeable or comfortable with some personal or academic challenge that had previously stymied them. Our hope was that we would discover more about our students, especially about how they become successful in their academic work. We also hoped to identify additional ways that the library might foster our students' academic growth and success.

We found that students face a variety of challenges that lead them into a growing maturity in four distinct but interrelated and mutually reinforcing areas. Students who describe themselves or are described by advisors or professors as successful or competent, have made significant strides in social, academic, emotional, and physical maturity. Students need to develop skills and ease in dealing with the procedural demands of campus and college life, such as finding good places to study and managing time, just as much as they need to develop academic skills and a sustained academic focus. Success in both of these areas is significantly influenced by how well they achieve awareness of their own personality and life circumstances, learn to balance their academic and non-academic relationships, and manage their personal physical and health needs, such as sleep, stress, and, in some cases, chronic illness.

Methodology
For the study, we engaged students, staff, and faculty members in three different research activities.

Panel Interviews of Resident Advisors
We conducted two panel interviews, one with

five and the other with seven resident advisors (RAs). To arrange these interviews, we contacted the director of Residential Life who provided names and e-mail addresses of RAs. We held panel interviews on two different days to accommodate the RAs' schedules. We compensated each RA with $20 and provided refreshments. The interviews were conducted by four team members, with one facilitating and the others providing assistance. We recorded and transcribed both panel interviews. (For the interview questions, see Appendix 5A.)

Advisor Interviews

We interviewed four pre-major advisors and four major advisors. Pre-major advisors are volunteers from across the campus, not necessarily faculty, who assist mainly freshmen and sophomores who have not yet declared their majors. The four pre-major advisors we interviewed were members of the library staff. We also interviewed four major advisors: three professors and a university administrator. Undergraduates are assigned a major advisor as soon as they formally declare a major. Team members were individually paired with advisors for these interviews. (For the interview questions, see Appendix 5B.)

Student Photo Interviews

The last step of our research was to ask students to take five specific photos around campus that exemplified aspects of their life on the campus. For example, we asked them to take photos of two things about the University that used to be hard and now seem easy. The participants sent us the pictures electronically before the interview, and then two of the team members interviewed each student. All interviews were recorded by digital voice recorder and transcribed by student assistants. Subjects received $20 for participation. (For the interview questions, see Appendix 5C.)

To cover the gamut of college experience we interviewed two freshmen, two sophomores, two juniors, two seniors, and a fifth-year undergraduate who was in our Take Five program.[2] We selected students randomly within each class with two recruitment strategies. First, we collected names of students during our annual Halloween party, which draws large numbers of undergraduates into the library. When this set of information did not provide enough appropriate study subjects at the time we needed their participation, we had a student assistant recruit the remaining students we needed to fill our "spectrum." This recruitment activity took place in non-library campus spaces in the course of one evening. Of the nine students in our photo study, only five students completed the interview task as planned, that is, by taking the requested photos in advance. The remaining four students were interviewed immediately upon recruitment, without having taken photographs.

Finally, we relied on data from a set of photo elicitation interviews conducted separately in which students took photos in response to a list of twenty questions, ranging from students' favorite places to do academic work to their favorite times of the day and even their favorite pair of shoes. The responses to these questions supplied us with a greater appreciation for the details of our students' lives as well as a clearer visual understanding of the things they carry and the places they go. (For the interview questions, see Appendix 5D.[3])

Academic Maturity: Developing Academic Skills and Focus

A passion, or strong intellectual interest, is a good indicator of a student's potential for academic success. Many of the students who chose their major or course of study to please parents or open doors to well-paying careers, rather than because of an intrinsic interest in the subject matter, seemed to lack the motivation needed to sustain the level of effort and follow-through required by the rigorous workload in college. One faculty advisor noted that the University now attracts a higher quality of student and he no longer has students who are lacking in intellectual ability but rather contends with students who are not motivated to do the work. Parental expectations can be an issue here, particularly in a student's early years, and one advisor noted that an advisee needed to "state her independence, move to something she's passionate about" to achieve academic success.

When students enter college, their career goals are often influenced by their parents' wishes or their own idealized notions, and, in many cases, these wishes and notions yield to a very different reality. For example, an academic advisor at the College Center for Academic Support told us that every year upwards of 40% of incoming freshmen express an interest in medicine and attend the information session during orientation. However, only around 8% of the graduating class apply to medical schools, and an even smaller 5% are actually accepted (University of Rochester, 2012).

Learning to Read Critically

One issue that arose repeatedly in interviews with advisors and undergraduates was the importance of the ability to read, study, and integrate materials for class. Advisors reported that some students lacked critical thinking skills and seemed more comfortable simply regurgitating what they learned rather than analyzing and integrating the material. Several students discussed the difficulty they had with assigned reading and understanding what they should be focusing on in their reading. One student said, "I missed the point. I just did the entire reading, but I've missed it because I wasn't reading for that." Another student explained the difficulty of working in a less structured environment than high school and having to study without

specific "prompts" to tell her what she should be looking for. In several of the cases, sometimes after receiving poor grades, the students began attending office hours, asking questions in class or working in peer groups.

Learning One's Own Working Style

Some students began working in peer groups to gain support in understanding course materials. One advisor, when noting that students need to develop an ability to solve problems, made the observation that "successful students often work together … they have study groups informally or more formally and they just stick together and approach the materials together and help each other." Working collaboratively often seemed to help students become better learners. On the other hand, some students emphasized the need to work independently in order to concentrate on the material. One student shared how he found quiet study spaces in the Science Library where he could spread his materials out on the desk. He told us that he could concentrate only when working alone at his own pace. We asked whether he ever worked with his peers. He told us that even when he worked next to his friend they did different things and did not interact with each other. Some students indicated that working independently in proximity to other students was part of their strategy to stay on task and not be distracted by other activities or thoughts.

Learning through Challenging Projects and in Real Contexts

Several students explained the processes by which they finally came to understand difficult concepts and course material. An engineering student described how he learned to use a popular engineering tool. At first it was confusing to use the tool because he had to learn a new computer language. However, when he had to use the tool in engineering courses over two years in real contexts, he became highly skilled, largely from watching videos and reading forums online. Other examples were students who learned a language abroad or a senior who learned to collect resources to write a senior history thesis. They noted that using the skills they learned in real contexts helped them to understand their material more clearly. They went through a sometimes painful learning process and finally mastered the subject, which boosted their academic self-esteem. In addition they became passionate about subjects after accomplishing difficult projects, even when they had been reluctant to take on the challenge at the beginning of the process.

Figure 5.1. MatLab: a complex engineering tool that can be mastered with practice

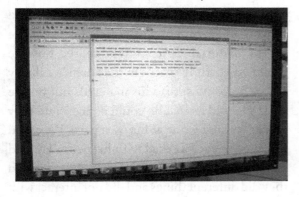

Learning to Find Academic Resources

The ability to find academic resources is another crucial skill for undergraduates. Students sometimes arrive in college with certain inhibitions that act as barriers to finding what they need. For example, some students will not approach a librarian to ask for help although this may be the simplest way forward. One student working on his senior thesis described trying to track down obscure foreign newspapers for his research. It was only after his conversation with a reference librarian that he discovered WorldCat and interlibrary loan, allowing him access to the material he needed. At other times, students hesitate to go into the stacks because they find

them intimidating or are confused by the library building's layout.

Another barrier may be the different schedules that librarians and students keep. Since our earlier studies of students indicated that many students use the library late at night (Clark, 2007; Bell & Unsworth, 2007), there is conflict between the times that students prefer to work and the times that the library is open and staffed. It often happens that students come to the library to locate academic resources only to find that reference and online chat services are closed.

Learning to Get Help

In addition to the library, the University has a considerable infrastructure to help students get the help they need for their academic life and decision making. Students appear to know and use services, such as the Writing Center, Career Center, and University academic advisors. However, many students seem to feel a lack of long-term academic mentorship and are unsure of how this can be resolved. It emerged that in some academic departments, students do not retain the same academic advisor as they progress through their program. One student described her experience as follows: "There's a list of like 10 advisors I can go to if I have a question, so then ... on different days of the week I'll go to a different person, but no one, I don't get to know anyone really well. And that's before I start classes, so I don't have someone in a department who's known me since freshman year or has seen me grow." Some faculty indicated that students do not regularly approach them for help. In one department, a faculty advisor indicated that when students declare a major, they fill out a piece of paper that outlines their courses for the major. Unless they deviate from that plan, they never need to visit an advisor again. He added, "For most of them, I'm not much of an advisor."

The advising procedures across academic departments are inconsistent and often do not seem to encourage a real relationship between the student and advisor. This is cause for strong concern as academic advisors play an important role in connecting students with faculty members and other important people. However, students indicated that the Career Center strives to develop long-term relationships with students, starting as early as the freshman year. At least two students were able to name their career center advisors.

Social Maturity: Dealing with the Campus and with College Life

Along with academic mastery, success in college depends on a broad range of non-academic factors that relate to the development of adult social competence. Adjustment to and integration within the social fabric of college life are just as important to student retention as academic factors (Gerdes & Mallinckrodt, 1994). We learned from faculty advisors that students are better prepared for college academics and are more likely to succeed at college if they are able to master the basic "rules." Some of these rules are actual regulations while others are rules of thumb or guidelines. Students must obey laws, such as the statutes against harassment, and university regulations, such as registering for classes or completing course work before specified deadlines. However,

there are numerous informal and sometimes unspoken rules and procedures that they must learn to follow in order to succeed, such as how and when to approach an instructor for help or where to talk and where to be quiet in the library.

Managing Daily Lives

Only a few incoming students, for example, those who have attended a boarding school, seem already to have learned how to take responsibility for the routines of their daily lives. Simple things, such as getting to bed at a reasonable hour, doing laundry, or being prepared for a meeting with an academic advisor, have to be learned. Other details also can be daunting, such as finding a classroom or mastering complicated dining and flex-spending plans. Students need to learn administrative skills and take on scheduling and problem-solving responsibilities that few have had to think about before because they had the services of parents to rely on. As one student said, "My mom spoiled me, growing up. I'll admit that. She definitely does a lot of things for me, that obviously, once I came here, she couldn't do those things for me at all. So, I think, yeah, I had an adjustment." Students continue to rely on their parents for guidance, but also begin to look to peers and other mentors for assistance in making decisions.

Figure 5.2. Developing new skill sets

Managing Time

Time management came up repeatedly in interviews with undergraduates, often in reference to their schedules. While their schedules had been designed for them in high school, many told us that they became responsible for planning and managing their own schedules in college. As one student explained, "When I was a freshman, I had a terrible time with time management and couldn't balance being in class versus socializing versus taking time to do homework … and so now I'm a senior and I've kind of got it figured out." Students showed us a variety of planners. Many seemed to prefer the print calendar, which they carried around with them all the time, while others used the Google calendar built into their university e-mail. Regardless of what kind of calendar they used, students seemed to realize that they needed a plan to stay organized and balance their tasks.

Figure 5.3. Students use print or online calendars to stay organized

Managing Space

Students not only have to manage their time, they also have to manage their work spaces. Some students prefer to work in groups while studying, even if that means sitting at a table full of friends, working on individual tasks. Other students prefer to work alone in quiet spaces where they will not be distracted by the environment or the activities of other people. The variety of work spaces offered by the library was a frequent topic in the student interviews. Students would describe when they "discovered" their work space or which space they preferred for a particular study style. For example, one student described finding the quiet space of the Periodical Reading Room while visiting a professor's office in the library. Other students never left the Gleason Library, a collaborative and relatively noisy work area within the library building. Many students seemed to find these spaces almost by accident, either tagging along with a friend or visiting a professor.

Students told us that they selected their work space largely on the basis of the type of work they intended to do. When they had to do homework, they seemed to choose from a great variety of spaces, many of them lively and collaborative, including their dorm and other non-library locations on campus. There seems to be a social aspect to doing homework, and students like the option to interact with classmates and friends while engaging in this activity. When students studied for tests they were more evenly divided between wanting to work in a noisier or quieter space. Still, they reported wanting to work in proximity to their friends. This may mean using group spaces even if they are working on individual tasks. However, when students needed to focus on writing papers, the majority chose to hide themselves away in the library stacks or in other quiet spaces, and the collaborative library spaces were rarely mentioned.

Balancing Social Life

While the students we spoke with seemed to take their academic work seriously, they also had recreational interests they wanted to pursue. Sports, fraternities and sororities, clubs, and part-time jobs all competed with class time and study time in their daily schedules. The students explained that it was a matter of finding the right balance among their academic and social activities. One

Figure 5.4. The quiet Periodical Reading Room, one student's favorite work space

student explained, "I thought it would be easier to join many clubs, and I realized that I can't diversify, I can't spread my time that easily. When I got here freshman year, I actually joined like 10 or 11 clubs." He explained that after that first semester he dropped nearly all of them because he realized he wanted to narrow his focus and concentrate on his academic work. Students experiment until they find a balance of work and play that is sustainable.

Learning from Role Models

As the first role models that freshmen encounter, resident advisors (RAs) and other student leaders can play a major role in helping incoming students adjust to academic life and begin to develop good habits. One RA said, "Being a presence on the hall … is a big deal. Showing them not just telling them what you do, but showing them what you do. Making an effort to go to the library and come back and show that you're having a social life and doing this, and exhibiting

that balance." RAs also help guide new students through their first social networking experiences on campus: By organizing hall meetings and activities, they introduce and encourage students to interact and build relationships with one another. This can often be a stepping stone to new interests, classes, and social activities. RAs and other peer leaders can be a strong early influence in helping undergraduates transition into the college environment.

Learning to Explore

One of the greatest requirements for success at college is to explore and ask questions. Whether it is taking a class outside of a chosen major, browsing a library shelf, showing up at a club informational meeting, or just taking a different route around campus, a lot of learning can take place outside of one's expected academic path. Exploring can mean making new friends, discovering new interests, and learning how best to interact with one's environment. Asking questions can be intimidating, especially when everything is new; one student learned that asking "How do I put money on my ID card?" was only part of the real question. It was only later that she learned that she also needed to ask how to put scholarship money on her card. However, by asking questions and exploring the college environment, students open themselves up to all sorts of possibilities.

Emotional Maturity: Managing Needs and Discovering Oneself

Interwoven with the academic and social maturation of undergraduates as they emerge into adulthood is an emotional maturation. For some this can be very intense. They may struggle with making their own decisions, reevaluating childhood goals, defining their own interests, and overcoming a fear of authority figures. Some may even have to stand up to their parents and assert their own agenda over their parents' long-held desires.

Becoming Comfortable with Choice

The new freedom that undergraduates have to choose their own curriculum, or even fashion their own majors, is both a significant attraction and a source of unease. Several advisors and some students spoke about how overwhelming this freedom of choice could be. There can be a strong underlying fear of making mistakes in selecting from the University of Rochester's open curriculum, even though this openness was what attracted them to the University in the first place. There is also the reality that for some students, success or even a strong interest in a subject in high school, does not predict success at college. Very few students come in with the understanding of what it takes to make adjustments when the reality of their skills and interests no longer agrees with who they thought they were and what they thought they would do.

Fearing Faculty

This road to self-discovery can have several ob-

Figure 5.5. Students select from an overwhelming number of choices

stacles. One advisor spoke about the panic that sets in for students who are surprised by how badly they did on their first major test and how they would resist their pre-major advisor's advice to talk to their professor. Academic advisors, RAs, and students spoke about students' reluctance, even fear, of talking to their professors, especially when they knew that they were not doing well. Various reasons were offered, such as being intimidated or not wanting to admit to floundering or feeling weak. Communication styles may also be a factor; one advisor observed that "this is a generation that uses [electronic] tools to communicate, and face-to-face communication is becoming more difficult for this generation." Students in large classes also seemed to be intimidated. Faculty members are often described by students as daunting or scary. One student said, "I thought professors are supposed to be these intimidating people ... that know everything and you are inferior because you are a student." And while most students eventually get over this, the fear of interacting runs deep. One student said of the professors who she had successfully interacted with, "They're the nicest ever, and even now, they're still intimidating. Yeah. But I still can't wrap my mind around it." This is consistent with what we learned from our interviews; students will first go to their peers, then to their teaching assistants (TAs), and finally (sometimes at the point of being summoned) to their professors.

Finding Role Models and Mentors

Once students conquer their misgivings about seeking help, they seem to find that connecting and working with others has a significant influence on academic success and on long-term career success, and for many it is fundamentally rooted in a growing emotional and social maturity. Many students mentioned having a role model, such as a coach, RA, professor, sorority sister, or, in one case, a cousin who helped the student adjust to life at the University of Rochester. One student described her sorority sisters as "older women that have been adjusted to campus already. They were there to kind of show me the ropes of how to approach certain social aspects, but also how to manage classes." Advisors also noticed how crucial these relationships could be to making a successful transition to life on campus. They described the bonds the students form with these role models and how they helped the students to figure out life on campus and life in general. Students told similar stories. One student said that he had intended to become a doctor but working as a TA for a faculty member in biology had moved him toward wanting to be a researcher. Another student characterized her relationship with an advisor in the Career Center as "brutally honest," allowing for truly meaningful discussions. One student, not included in the study, wrote eloquently in the student newspaper about his transformation from someone who was intimidated by the academic prowess of the professors, graduate students, and upperclassmen to someone who realized that it took the help of a whole community to begin to master the discipline (Khaitan, 2010). Role models, in both academic and social capacities, can have a life-changing impact on students.

Discovering One's Passion

Getting settled in to campus and academic life is only the beginning. While a few students manage to successfully follow the academic path that they originally envisioned, many students find that they need to change or refine their academic and career focus. Having to change one's view of oneself can be challenging. Professors and advisors spoke about the slowness with which pre-med students came to grips with this central conflict; others spoke about how some students actually needed time away from the university to make the commitment to the work that was required of them in order to succeed. Sometimes there are additional challenges. At least one advisor spoke of students that would not let go of their biology major until the third or fourth semester at which point they had little experience with alternative disciplines, making it difficult to comfortably fashion a new major. For other students, there is the burden of expectations. Sometimes these are their own self-expectations and other times they are the expectations (real or perceived) of their parents. Advisors spoke of students who worried about how to tell their parents about their new choices and goals. One student had the understanding that if he picked a career path with lower-income expectations he would need to transfer to a less expensive school.

The discovery of where one's passions and talents lie should help in choosing a curriculum that can bring those interests and skills into a reasonable life pursuit. This discovery may also require a student to achieve a greater degree of self-awareness and to negotiate his or her identity and goals with family members who have harbored different hopes. It was clear that when students came to the point of actually speaking with their parents about their career expectations, it was a milestone in both their self-identity and their level of maturity. Sometimes these conver-

sations were prompted by the student's inability to get the grades necessary for academic success within a given major, and sometimes it was more a matter of what the student really loved.

Part of the transformation into a college student and young adult is the ability to recognize one's own interests, make one's own decisions, and stand up for them. One advisor explained how involved some parents are with their children's academic choices: "We're working on their schedule for the next semester, and their instinct is to call Mom. And I have to say, 'No, put the phone down. We're not going to call Mom right now.'" However, a strong relationship between parents and students is not necessarily a bad thing. One advisor noted that successful students "still had a strong connection with their parents, but they seem to have formed a sense of their own empowerment. So they were still very much in communication with the parents, but they knew that their decisions were theirs to make."

The sooner students understand where their true interests lie, the sooner they seem to become successful students. One RA observed that the students who are resistant to change struggle the most. The level and intensity of the work required at the University of Rochester is only sustain-

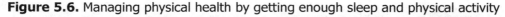

Figure 5.6. Managing physical health by getting enough sleep and physical activity

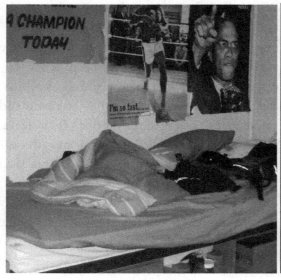

able if one is completely committed. Academic advisors spoke about how they can almost see the students change physically when they find something they are passionate about—that is when they know that students have "got it."

Physical Maturity: Taking Care of One's Physical and Health Needs

The management of the body's needs is another area in which students need to mature in order to do well in college. Students must learn to feed themselves adequately and at regular intervals, they must learn how to manage their schedules so that they get enough sleep, and they must learn how to deal with minor and major illness when they are on their own. For some students, the management of chronic conditions, such as diabetes or depression, is such a challenge that their academic work may be affected. For these students especially, attaining a degree of maturity that supports the calm and effective care of one's body takes some time and can delay the adjustment to college life.

Conclusion

In general, we learned that the process of "learning the ropes" is one of maturation in four distinct but interrelated and mutually reinforcing areas. Students who describe themselves or are described by advisors or professors as successful or competent have made significant strides in these four areas:

1. Academic maturity: developing a sustained academic focus along with academic skills essential to the college environment
2. Social maturity: developing skill and ease in dealing with procedural demands of campus and college life, such as finding good places to study and managing time
3. Emotional maturity: managing academic and non-academic relationships, achieving self-awareness of personality and life circumstances

4. Physical maturity: managing personal physical and health needs, such as getting enough sleep, managing stress, and, in some cases, treatment for chronic illness

Future Directions

Based on our findings, we have developed several ideas for creating the relationships, spaces, and framework of support that students need to succeed.

Creating Relationships

After speaking with students, RAs and advisors, we realize how critical relationships are to helping students develop a sense of community and begin to transition into being successful students. Based on what we have learned, we came up with some ideas to build on and strengthen relationships with and among undergraduates.

Serve as Mentors

We can develop a stronger subject librarian presence in classrooms (both in person and online) with the intention of creating a model of consistent mentorship in the library. For example, we can sit in on classroom lessons and participate in the discussions, with the intention of being a familiar face that students can turn to for help afterwards. As students indicated that they often feel uncomfortable talking to faculty for the first time, they may be more comfortable approaching librarians.

To build relationships with students, we can reach out to student organizations to collaborate on activities, such as book displays and exhibits in the library. This will allow students the chance to promote their clubs, and librarians the chance to play a supporting role in club activities, if appropriate.

More library staff can be encouraged to volunteer as pre-major advisors. Pre-major advisors develop a more complete sense of the issues students are facing as they transition on campus, better enabling them to help students with their research. As an added bonus, when advisees seek guidance, they would visit the library and get to know a librarian while working on their academic schedules.

There are opportunities beyond that of pre-major advisors that create a natural mentoring role for librarians. In 100-level courses, librarians could go beyond helping students find library resources and play a role in easing students' anxiety of not knowing how to begin a research assignment, ask critical questions, or connect sources with their own work.

Create Reasons to Visit the Library

We discovered that many students seem to find the library by accident, when they tag along with a friend or visit a professor who has an office in the library building. To increase the chance of "accidental" discovery, we could create more opportunities for students to find us. One way would be to host freshmen-level classes and TA-review sessions in the library. This could bring students into the building and introduce them to the different library spaces and faces that are available to them. Another way would be to implement low-barrier, game-like orientation activities, such as a freshmen scavenger hunt. With a modest prize and the promise of a fun activity, students may be willing to explore the library on their own.

Reward Questions

If a student stops by a library desk and asks a question, even if it is just a printing problem or directions for the restroom, we could reward such inquisitive behavior with a small token of thanks. This may not be sustainable all year long, but if it is implemented early in the semester, rewards may make an impression and encourage students to return to the desk later on when they have real research questions. This may also help

break the barrier students feel with figures of authority, especially those behind a desk. Students often do not bring their research queries to reference librarians because (1) they do not think of librarians as a solution to their problems; and (2) they often believe they know how to research without help. If we can catch them early on with superficial questions, then they may think of us later when they have more substantial questions.

Share Stories of Success

During our interviews we found many examples of students who had "learned the ropes" and figured things out over time. It may be worthwhile to talk to some of these students (RAs, student leaders) and profile them in relation to the library. Sharing their stories on the library website, on Facebook, or in other places where students gather may make studying in the library or approaching a librarian more realistic for new students. Just as profiles of students are used in college brochures, the library could share stories of how successful students discovered interlibrary loan, used Medline for the first time, or got help from a reference librarian while writing an important paper.

Extend Chat Service and Implement Emerging Technology

Currently we offer live chat service from 9:00 a.m. to 5:00 p.m. and reference desk service from 9:00 a.m. to 10:00 p.m. From our previous studies and the interviews we conducted this time, we realized that we need to match librarian availability more closely to times of day, week, and semester that students are most likely to need help with information seeking. This may be easiest to address by increasing online chat hours since students are frequently working in the wee hours. To increase chat hours, we may consider allowing librarians to work from home at night and during the weekend. Additionally, we may try to collaborate with other academic libraries in different time zones or create an internship for library science graduate students to work as chat operators, offering 24/7 online reference services.

Implementation of emerging technology to enable timely and effective communication, such as mobile computing and visual teleconferencing (e.g., Skype) for both students and librarians can be helpful. We may provide a smart phone or an iPad with data plan for the librarians on duty so they can provide answering service remotely after office hours.

Creating Spaces

Students love our space. They told us numerous times how they found "their" area of the library or where they do different kinds of studying. They may not always use our resources, but they love to use our space. To better match our space to their needs, here are a few ideas:

Become the "Brain" on Campus

We can showcase the library as an informational and intellectual center of the campus. By sponsoring talks that feature interesting, eminent faculty members discussing what they do and how they found themselves intellectually, the library clearly becomes the "brain" on campus. The library can also become the place where students learn about exciting events, lectures, and what research is happening on the campus and in the community, not just from paper flyers but also from interactive displays.

Create Space for Students to Form Relationships

We could display the work of visiting researchers and speakers and encourage students to attend events where they can meet these people and learn about their work. Sponsoring casual get-togethers, such as a storytelling swap and brief "How I Became a Researcher" presentations, may help students overcome their reluctance to interact with faculty members and university

researchers and even provide an incubator for developing relationships with otherwise intimidating authority figures.

Provide More Spaces

We can provide more spaces for students to spread out and stick around in the library and on campus. We have been renovating and expanding study spaces in the library and providing more tables and study carrels over the last 10 years. We will continue to assess the spaces in the library since larger parts of the collection will become available electronically and we will be able to free up more space in the stacks. We can also accommodate students' technology needs, for example, more electrical outlets for laptops and smart phones in the library.

Create Specialized Spaces

We could provide and publicize different kinds of spaces for students who require different types of accommodation, such as wheelchair-height desks, monitors modified for those with low vision, or other equipment that the Office of Disabilities might suggest.

Create a Framework of Support

In addition to working directly with students to foster good working relationships and listening for how to better tailor our physical spaces to meet students' needs, we can also improve on some of the underlying framework that supports success in those endeavors by fostering better relationships with RAs and making library staff more aware of students' growth and maturity during their time at college.

Develop Relationships with RAs

Librarians already work with professors and instructors to encourage them to model and promote the use of the libraries and their staff. In the same way, librarians might develop relationships with RAs to better connect undergraduates with the library. Although they are students, RAs are seen as authority figures and often as role models. For freshmen, RAs are the first "older" students they encounter and the first individuals to whom they look for guidance and advice. Several RAs told us how they try to set an example for their residents by actively studying in the library and posting their study schedules outside their doors. Librarians could work directly with RAs, creating designated study times for certain halls in desirable study areas, encouraging entire floors to study together in the library. RAs are often looking for hall activities to do with their residents as a means of socializing and bonding; the library should look for ways to develop these activities in the library.

Enable Staff to Work Better with Students

Reference staff members in particular have had a sense that asking for help can be stressful for any-

one. Our research has deepened our awareness of the types, levels, and potential timing of the stress that undergraduates experience. There is value in making library staff aware of the emotional adjustments and stress in students' lives, which may encourage staff to be even more compassionate and understanding, leading to more thoughtful interactions with students. These interactions could range from being able to provide support and practical advice on how to approach intimidating instructors to something as simple and as powerful as a friendly and welcoming manner. Additionally, deepened understanding could create an awareness of possible warning signs that a student needs the specialized help of a professor or even a counselor. This training, when coupled with the knowledge of how and to whom the student might be referred, could be useful in getting a student through a particularly difficult transition.

Appendix 5A. Questions Used in Panel Interviews with Residence Advisors

1. What are the biggest obstacles that students encounter as entering freshmen?
2. What has proved to be the best way to help these students, in your experience?
3. Describe ways freshmen change going from first semester into second semester.
4. What about the obstacles that returning students (sophomores, juniors) encounter? And the best ways to help them?
5. How do the students figure out a sustainable balance between academic work and the rest of their campus lives?
6. Tell us about students who you think do not make a good adjustment. Describe students who do.
7. Do transfer students have special problems? What have you learned about good and bad transitions for transfer students?
8. Based on your experiences in Residential Life, what would you say are the best things that faculty and staff could do to help students do well academically? How does this relate to students' lives in general?
9. In what ways does the University of Rochester help students adjust to college life? Can you suggest other things that would be useful for the students?
10. If you could give incoming freshmen one critical piece of advice, what would that be?

Appendix 5B. Questions Used in Interviews with Pre-major Advisors and Major Advisors

1. Can you give us a couple of examples of students who were "clueless" about their academic work? What happened? What was the consequence? What did the student learn?

2. Can you give us a couple of examples of students who "figured college out"? What happened? What did the student learn? How was the student different afterwards?

3. What have you learned about "clueless" students?

4. What have you learned about students who have "figured college out"?

Appendix 5C. Questions Asked in the Photo Interviews

Instructions to student:

- Think of two things about the University of Rochester that used to be hard to impossible and now seems easy. Take pictures to represent both of these things.
- Think of two times that you were confused about some academic work or a resource you were using and then later "got it." Take a picture to illustrate both times.
- Take a picture that captures something you want to become.

E-mail or bring the pictures to us and we will talk about them in the interview.

Basic questions for the interview:

1. Let's look at a picture of something that was hard to do but now seems easy. What's in this picture? What was hard? How did it become easy? (Repeat with next picture.)

2. Let's look at a picture of when you "got it." What happened? What did you learn? How did that happen? (Repeat for final picture.) (Prompt: How have you changed as a student? What's different? When do you think this change happened? What contributed to it?)

3. Can you tell us about two people who have made your adjustment to college life easier? (There are no photos for this question.)

4. Let's look at the picture that represents what you want to become. Tell me about this. (Prompt: Are there any people who have provided an example to you, or who have helped you move toward what you want to become?)

Appendix 5D. Photo Elicitation Interview

Take the following photos. Mark the order of the photo in the space provided. Bring the camera back at the scheduled time for your interview.

The computer you use in the library, showing its surroundings

All the stuff you take to class

Something that you would call "high tech"

Something really weird

The place you keep your books

Your communication devices

A picture of your room, showing your computer

Another view of your room

How you schedule your time or keep track of your work

Your favorite part of the day

The tools you use for writing assignments

The things you always carry with you

Something you can't live without

A place in the library that you avoid or where you feel lost

A place on campus that you avoid or where you feel lost

A great place to do homework

Another great place to do homework

A great place to work on a paper

Another great place to work on a paper

A great place to study for a test or a quiz

Another great place to study for a test or a quiz

Your favorite shoes

Interview Instrument:
View the photographs with the student, asking about the photographs to elicit details of the student's work practices.

Notes

1. The team included Suzanne Bell, Vicki Burns, Nancy Foster, Kenn Harper, Mari Lenoe, and Marcy Strong.

2. The Take Five program enables a small number of students to pursue studies at no additional cost in fields of special interest outside of their majors. For more information about this program, see http://www.rochester.edu/college/CCAS/students/opportunities/takefive/.

3. See Chapter 4, "Picture My Work," for a review of the findings of the photo elicitation interviews.

References

Arnett, J.J. (2004). *Emerging adulthood: The winding road from the late teens through the twenties.* New York, NY: Oxford University Press.

Bell, S. & Unsworth, A. (2007). Night owl librarians: Shifting the reference clock. In N.F. Foster & S. Gibbons (Eds.), *Studying students: The undergraduate research project at the University of Rochester* (pp. 16–19). Chicago, IL: Association of College and Research Libraries.

Clark, K. (2007). Mapping diaries, or where do they go all day? In N.F. Foster & S. Gibbons (Eds.), *Studying students: The undergraduate research project at the University of Rochester* (pp. 48–54). Chicago, IL: Association of College and Research Libraries.

Khaitan, D. (2010, September 12). Personal recollections on the POA Library. *Campus Times.* Retrieved from http://www.campustimes.org/2010/04/15/personal-recollections-on-the-poa-Library/

Foster, N.F. & Gibbons, S. (Eds.) (2007). *Studying students: The undergraduate research project at the University of Rochester.* Retrieved from UR Research website: http://hdl.handle.net/1802/7520

Gerdes, H. & Mallinckrodt, B. (1994). Emotional, social, and academic adjustment of college students: A longitudinal study of retention. *Journal of Counseling & Development, 72*(3), 281–288.

University of Rochester. (2012). *2011–12 fact sheet.* Retrieved from http://enrollment.rochester.edu/admissions/res/pdf/factsheet.pdf

chapter six. "Whatever Works": Finding Trusted Information

Helen Anderson and Sarah Sexstone

How do faculty, students, and librarians look for information when it matters deeply to them? What are the similarities and differences in the research processes used by faculty, students, and librarians? Would the answers help us evaluate whether the support that we offer students through our programs and services is aligned with the processes used by serious researchers? These questions came up after the publication of *Studying Students: The Undergraduate Research Project at the University of Rochester* (Foster & Gibbons, 2007), which detailed the results of the Libraries' initial Undergraduate Research project. We wanted to identify changes we could make to the ways that librarians provide research support to students.

Methodology

When the Undergraduate Refresher project began in 2011, the Finding Trusted Information sub-team was one of four groups established to investigate questions that had occurred to us since the previous study.[1] We conducted interviews with eight undergraduate students, ten faculty members, and four librarians. We interviewed sophomore, junior, and senior undergraduates in science, social science, and humanities majors. The faculty represented a variety of disciplines, including anthropology, education, engineering, English, and mathematics.

We recognized that people conduct research in many different locations and situations, but we wanted to conduct the interviews in settings where the subjects would feel comfortable. The librarian and faculty interviews were held at their desks on campus. We interviewed the students in a quiet room in the library. A laptop was offered for their use, but we made it clear that they were free to work on their own devices. Interviews typically involved two people from our research team; one person introduced and conducted the interview and the other operated the equipment, acting as an observer and occasionally participating. All interviews were captured on videotape and audiotape. They lasted between half an hour and an hour in length. Later, our group analyzed and coded the printed transcripts and co-viewed the tapes, capturing our observations and ideas for possible action items on sticky notes as they occurred to us. These notes were later typed up and shared with the group. This was followed up by a presentation at our monthly staff meeting, discussions with smaller groups of staff, and a brown bag lunch.

We asked each subject to search for something that they really cared about, for which they really needed an answer they could trust, and allowed each of them to talk about whatever topic or information need that occurred to them in response to our questions. This provided a strong common thread across the three groups. Our assumption was that when people look for information that is of great personal interest to them, they will work hard and creatively to find the most reliable answer, the most usable information. In follow-up questions we asked each subject to tell us about similar searches they had done recently with the idea that this might provide us with additional, corroborating or contrasting, data. (See the Appendix 6A for the full list of questions.)

Students' Information Seeking

We asked students to identify a current information need related to a matter of personal value and interest, encouraging them to choose a topic on which they needed accurate information that they could trust.

The students then searched for information on such topics as pet health, current events, a play that was about to be performed, music, and the environment, among others. Most of the students used the Internet exclusively to find trusted information; however, there were exceptions. During one interview, a sophomore texted another student, a senior, whose opinion she valued: "She's smarter; she's a senior so she actually knows what she's doing." She received a response and used what she learned to modify her Internet search. Another student showed us books that he had taken from a topical display in the library just prior to the interview. He had identified them as possibly useful for his senior thesis and leafed through them. He pointed out chapters on topics of interest to him, the names that he was familiar with in footnotes, and the index at the back of a book.

Students tried to evaluate the credibility and reliability of the information they found on the Internet, but they did not always show sophistication in examining the sources they found. To find information quickly, students generally started with Google. Some students established authority by checking multiple sites to see if they all said the same thing, or by seeking information from people they knew, such as their professor or from an acknowledged expert. Other students simply considered the nature of the site where they found the information. For example, one student considered a network news site to be a trusted source for news and did not seek further corroboration.

The students we interviewed commonly identified information as trustworthy if it came from someone they knew and regarded as intel-

ligent or well informed. They looked for information on blogs, music sites, and social networking sites. They trusted information from people who had posted reliably in the past or from people they knew personally.

When they were telling us about recent searches they had done, students did talk about using library resources such as the Voyager catalog in addition to other institutional and commercial websites, for example, the University of Rochester website, Wikipedia, and Amazon. One student mentioned using WikiLeaks. Some spoke about visiting places on campus to find specific information, such as the Health Center or Career Center. Others talked about leaving campus to speak with people in the surrounding neighborhoods or to attend music performances to learn about new music.

All of the students demonstrated what we call a "whatever works" approach. They tried multiple strategies and used the web in many different ways. If one approach did not work, they would quickly try another—utilizing social networking sites to find information on current events or music; using the library or personal collections; and using RSS feeds, blogs, and news sites. Students communicated with people they knew or with experts either in person or through websites. They acknowledged professors, librarians, family, friends, conference presenters, and medical professionals as trusted sources of information and recommendations. They depended heavily on personal recommendations from people they trust, especially their friends, professors, bloggers, online reviewers, and music critics.

Faculty's Expectations of Students

Faculty told us that they expect undergraduates to know how to find books in the library catalog by author and title, to be able to use an academic database and Google Scholar, and to follow up on footnotes and references. They expect graduate students to be more sophisticated at finding readings, understanding more complex research, and producing original research of their own. They expect them to learn which journals to follow and to develop an analytical approach to scholarly literature.

They reported that they devote time to showing graduate students how to use databases, examine the reliability of a source, find bibliographies, and cite literature properly. Several faculty mentioned working with librarians to do these things. They also reported spending time with undergraduate students. Two of the faculty members we interviewed told us they give undergraduates the literature that they want them to read and do not expect them to identify relevant sources on their own or through the library. Two faculty members expressed more concern that students develop critical reading skills rather than library skills. One reported that his primary objective, particularly with freshmen, is simply to get them to read a book. Another said that he wants them to "hear what's going on, on the page." A few reported that they believe that students are far more skilled than they are at finding information using computers, cell phones, and related technologies. Even when providing support to graduates and undergraduates, faculty confess that they really do not know how students become proficient researchers, saying that it "just happens," or that it happens "by osmosis."

Some faculty told us they were frustrated that students do not understand how their topics relate to major issues and research in their fields. Some expressed nostalgia for the days of print and framed this as a generational or faculty-student difference. We thought this might be a sign of faculty frustration over the explosive growth of publication in scholarly fields and the difficulties this poses to teaching and research in the age of the Internet.

Librarians' Expectations of Students

The four librarians we interviewed reported that they have low expectations for freshmen in terms of library use. One commented that first year students are "a clean slate." However, most of the librarians did recognize that there is a lot of variation among students and that much depends on their library and research experiences in high school. One librarian reported surprise on learning, while teaching a library session, that the students already knew the difference between popular and scholarly journals. Some librarians said that while the students are looking for resources, they work alongside them to find good leads so that students will not be discouraged if they are not successful.

Seniors are a different matter. Most of the librarians we interviewed said that they expect seniors to be able to search the major databases in their field and be able to evaluate sources well. They should be able to locate references from citation lists and be familiar with the important authors and literature in the fields they are majoring in. The librarians reported that they believe that students develop strong interests over time and learn how to find and cite information, although they are not sure exactly how that happens.[2]

The librarians reported they expect that graduate students are even more advanced than college seniors and do not need the same kind of help undergraduates need. They said that over the course of their training, graduate students develop an array of library research strategies, although they did not know exactly how or when the student develop this expertise. The librarians said that students figure out what their professors want and then conduct their research in a largely self-sufficient manner. Librarians reported that they see their roles shifting from "gatekeeper" to "facilitator" in connection with their work with faculty and students at all levels.

Faculty's Information Seeking

We asked faculty to tell us about their non-academic interests and then asked them to look for information in one or more of these areas. They searched for information on a range of topics, including house remodeling, coins, sports, restaurants, pet health, and local culture. Several showed difficulty with identifying interests that were unrelated to their academic work.

In observing faculty as they sought information, we noted similarities to the processes used by students. Faculty also used a "whatever works" approach to finding trusted information. One person used a phone app. Another decided that he would talk to colleagues. Otherwise they all used their computers to search for information. They often used Google as a starting point to get to a known site by typing in a keyword plus the word "wiki" to reach a Wikipedia entry. We also saw faculty use their own search history to navigate back to a previously identified site. They visited government sites, restaurant sites, and RocWiki, a site for local information about Rochester, New York. When faculty told us about searches that they had conducted prior to the interview, they often mentioned Google, Google Scholar, and Wikipedia. One person told us how she used Facebook for conversations about interesting and important political issues, and one talked about researching music on YouTube.

Faculty also told us about other methods they had used. Some of these involved going to a University of Rochester library and using the library's website, using public and personal libraries, or purchasing books. They told us about their connections to organizations and how they used the newsletters and webpages of these organizations as well as interchanges with fellow members. Some talked about taking classes and learning from instructors. Faculty also talked about using book reviews, specifically the *New York Times Book Review* and *The New Yorker* as well as reviews from Amazon. In the case of Amazon, they either talked about assessing the validity of the reviews or referred to them as "ethnography on the cheap." The methods most often mentioned involved seeking information and advice from colleagues and other experts. This might include attending meetings or conferences, whether academic or not; learning about other people's research projects; and getting in touch with academic colleagues, fellow enthusiasts, or local experts through e-mail, telephone calls, and personal visits.

Librarians' Information Seeking

We asked librarians to find information while we observed them and to tell us about recent occasions on which they had to find information on topics with personal meaning for them. We were particularly interested in the different strategies that librarians used when they had a personal stake in the richness and accuracy of the answers. Search strategies were not at all formulaic but instead were extremely varied: Librarians used whatever searching strategy seemed to work just as the students and faculty did. Some started with keyword searches, others searched for particular authors or experts, starting broadly and narrowing down results, using an asterisk as a wildcard, and so on.

The librarians looked for information on a variety of topics, including treatment of sports injuries, antiques, hiking trails, medical topics, and music. They searched sources ranging from academic resources (ISI Web of Science and PLOS) to popular but credible websites (Mayo Clinic, ABE Books) to recreational sites (YouTube, music sites) to commercial or retail sites. One librarian showed us an article received from a trusted individual, while others said they trusted certain sites because of the experts that contributed to them.

Similarly, when librarians told us about recent searches on topics of particular interest to them that they had done prior to the interview, they mentioned using Google, WorldCat, Voyager, and a variety of databases as well as non-academic websites. They also mentioned using books, either from their personal collections or borrowed from friends or the library. One person told us about visiting a museum collection to find out more about items she was collecting. In several cases, we heard about librarians following up on leads from experts of one kind or another, whether collectors, presenters at conferences, museum docents, teachers, or other librarians.

Librarians did not show a distinct preference for library resources or follow any consistent set of steps for seeking information. Like the students and faculty, librarians used a "whatever works" approach. One librarian called his own searching "not very sophisticated" and another voiced a very similar sentiment. Regardless of the sophistication of the searching strategy, we saw that librarians were able to find good information using a wide range of strategies. They also demonstrated a continuous process of assessing and then accepting or rejecting the information they found, although in fairly informal and non-rigorous ways.

Comparing Student, Librarian, and Faculty Processes

All three groups used of a variety of information seeking techniques. Everyone we observed used Google, Amazon, and Wikipedia heavily. They also used their own libraries and, especially notable, referred to personal connections and experts. Everyone we interviewed recognized that they must assess the credibility of information they find on websites, but they exhibited a great deal of variation in how much and how well they did this. In general, we found that those who had developed a greater familiarity with their subject—both in terms of knowledge and in terms of the tools and resources available—were better able to assess the reliability of the information they found on the web.

We were particularly interested in how faculty find information on topics that are of great personal interest to them because we wanted to get a sense of how they find things when they have a personal stake in the information seeking process. Indeed, we took the same approach with all three groups in order to have comparable data. Our assumption was that when people look for information that is of great personal interest and importance, they will work hard and be creative, seeking the best, most reliable, and most usable information. We took this as one of the most important contexts of information seeking, although we recognize that most of what we saw was not of life-or-death importance. As one professor told us, faculty members apply different standards to information sought in connection with hobbies than they do to information sought for use in an academic publication.

Interestingly, librarians do not follow professionally prescribed routines in seeking information related to their personal interests. Indeed, librarians resemble faculty, drawing from a large toolkit and shifting among strategies until they find one that works. Two librarians explicitly described this approach as "unsophisticated" or "not quite up to snuff," but our impression is that this iterative, "whatever works" method is, in fact, the method of choice for academics whose research abilities are acknowledged as strong.

Findings

Students, librarians, and faculty members use a similar "whatever works" process to find information that is personally interesting to them. This process is an iterative one of trial and error. It draws on a personal set of tools and resources that the individual builds up over time and uses when needed. The process is heavily electronic but also includes print resources, people resources, and real-world activity.

All three groups also use prior information to assess new information. They are more or less successful depending on how well they already know the area they are researching. Across the board, people who do not already know a lot about what they are researching are at greater risk of accepting bad information as good information. In other words, accrued knowledge helps people assess new information. Those who have built up a strong basis of information and a set of diverse information-finding tools show greater skill at finding numerous sources of precise, reliable information.

Historically, the "whatever works" method resembles past practice, except that there are now many more tools and resources and they are constantly changing and developing. Whereas in the past, both subject specific and general knowledge indexes and resources retained the same organization and focus for decades, now interfaces multiply and change almost daily. It is no longer enough to learn how to use a tool once. It may appear and work entirely differently the next time you use it.

Primary material that was once accessible only by those who were able and willing to travel thousands of miles is easily available on the desktop, sometimes via multiple interfaces; there is much more content for researchers to wade through and evaluate. Peer-reviewed articles and other traditional scholarly materials are joined on the Internet by a plethora of material authored by non-specialists. This reality challenges developing scholars who must locate, digest, assess, and decide to discard or retain new sources of information.

Even though people feel that they are successful searchers and find what they need, they could benefit from learning about more tools and resources or developing skill at using those tools and resources more effectively. As content proliferates and the speed of change accelerates, there is a need for librarians to continuously adjust their teaching strategies and keep the library web presence up to date and relevant. In addi-

tion to keeping up with the changes in licensed databases and tools, librarians must also keep up with freely available resources, such as Google Scholar, Wikipedia, and so on.

Reinforcing and supporting the "whatever works" approach to finding and evaluating reliable information should be our focus in all our interactions with researchers, whether, in person, in library workshops or classes, or through website and OPAC design. Because we work closely with researchers at all levels, librarians are well positioned to work with publishers and producers of databases to develop information resources that support this process, while at the same time remembering that faculty sometimes just want students to use assigned course readings and to focus on reading deeply, attentively, and critically. Students do not always need to go out and find more resources.

While faculty and librarians know that college students come in with low-level research skills and that advanced graduate students have excellent skills, they are challenged to find effective ways to help students progress in their development. This research suggests that the library may have untapped opportunities to help students become better researchers by creating a student-faculty-librarian link in non-academic areas.

Such a link might provide students with opportunities to see how other people with similar interests pursue information related to those interests and provide them with an opportunity to see librarians as experts who can help them develop their research skills. It could help them develop knowledge of information tools and resources that would be helpful in their academic work because the process is the same, whether the interest is academic, personal, or recreational. Librarians might investigate opportunities to participate in the non-standard communication, for example, on lists or blogs that students and professors organize informally around academic interests.

Possible Actions

Based on our analysis of the interviews and brainstorming with colleagues, we are considering a number of possible actions in our library. As stated earlier, we have already sponsored co-viewing and discussion of the "whatever works" research process that we identified and discussed its implications for librarian practices. We have encouraged library staff to share and discuss new ways of doing research, especially ways that are learned from faculty and students. We are contemplating whether faculty and librarians could share their own research strategies and processes with students, perhaps in a way that is focused on mutual interests.

We are exploring ways for librarians to participate in informal, web-based communications about course-related issues with faculty and students, such as those that take place on lists, blogs, or Facebook. This kind of participation might support "finding the moment" to help students and faculty become better researchers. Technologies and media might include an "Ask a Librarian" blog or listserv, Facebook or Twitter accounts, or a Twitter hash mark for "trusted sources."

We are also investigating the continuation of relationships developed during library sessions with students and creating more outreach explicitly and specifically to faculty by adding other tools to enhance communication between faculty and subject librarians. We are also exploring other means of building the faculty-student-librarian relationship, such as finding more ways to get faculty to bring students to the library and having tips and guides available for students doing independent searches. One of the benefits of building these relationships is that they may provide students with good models for evaluating information. We want to help students compensate for their relative lack of knowledge and difficulty in assessing sources by encouraging them to use the "peer review/scholarly" filter in databases, a filter that will make more sense once students have become acquainted with the peer reviewer role performed by faculty members they already know.

Appendix 6A. Interview Questions

Note: We allowed all individuals to talk about whatever they wanted in response to these questions.

Undergraduate Student Interviews

- We want to know how you find out information when you have to find information you can trust. Is there an area or topic that you need to find out about or a question that you have to answer that is not related to work? Was there recently? We want either to follow you as you work on getting the information or have you draw a picture of what you did when you got the information.

- What are you studying? What do you think you'll do next year? How about after graduation? Do you have some ideas about what you might do with your life? What kind of work would you like to do? What do you think you might be doing with your time in your life after college?

Faculty Interviews

- We want to know how you find out information when you have to find information you can trust. Is there an area or topic that you need to find out about or a question that you have to answer that is not related to work? Was there recently? We want either to follow you as you work on getting the information or have you draw a picture of what you did when you got the information.

- What do you expect an entering freshman to know about finding books and articles for a research paper or research-based assignment?

- Can you tell us how you think students learn to find books and articles for research papers and research-based assignments?

- What do you expect an entering graduate student to know about finding books and articles for a research paper? Tell us something about how you imagine the student learned how to do that.

- What do you expect a PhD student to know about creating a bibliography for exams or the dissertation? Tell us how you imagine the student learned how to do that.

Librarian Interviews

- We want to know how you find information when you have to find information you can trust. Is there an area or topic that you need to find out about or a question that you have to answer that is not related to work? Was there recently? We want either to follow you as you work on getting the information or have you draw a picture of what you did when you got the information.

- What do you expect an entering freshman to know about finding books and articles for a research paper or research-based assignment?

- What you expect entering and advanced graduate students to know about finding books and articles for a research paper?

Notes

1. This sub-team included Helen Anderson, Nancy Foster, Kathy McGowan, Harish Nayak, and Sarah Sexstone.

2. Concurrent with the study described in this chapter, another sub-team investigated the way students in our university "learn the ropes." Their findings, which have been shared with librarians and library staff, have provided valuable insight into how students develop strong academic interests and the competence to pursue them. See Chapter 5, "Learning the Ropes," for further information about this sub-study.

References

Foster, N.F. & Gibbons, S. (Eds.) (2007). *Studying students: The undergraduate research project at the University of Rochester.* Retrieved from UR Research website: http://hdl.handle.net/1802/7520

chapter seven. **Research as Connection**

Nancy Fried Foster

People make information from anything in the world, but they get information from other people. People who do research understand this better as time goes by; they expand their access to information by cultivating their networks. People, living and dead, here and away, talk about their work in person, in presentations, in published work. Along with the books themselves and other products of this talk, they constitute a network of authors who are in scholarly communication with each other. In this chapter, I explore what we have learned about the work practices of academic researchers at all levels, from undergraduates to librarians and eminent scholars.[1] Our studies show that all researchers use a large number of means to get the information they need but no other means approaches the importance of consultation of each other.[2] I conclude by arguing that the *ad hoc* methods used by more experienced researchers would be most helpful for novice researchers to learn, starting with the knowledge that real people write the books and articles that look like random objects when they are found in a library catalog.

Researchers in Real Life

To participate in an academic community is to witness what seems like continuous engagement on the part of researchers in their projects. Researchers may claim that they can "turn it off," but they always seem to have their projects on at least a low simmer. The moment they happen upon anything even remotely related to their topics, up goes the heat.

Here is a very ordinary example. Six people, three of them actively engaged in research,

relax over dinner. One guest, a medical doctor, works in community medicine. Another, an anthropologist, shares the doctor's interest in the history and politics of food. The doctor wonders whether there are any books about corn that would be similar to the recent books on cod and potatoes. "Have you seen *Corn and Capitalism*?" asks the anthropologist. "I'll send you the reference."

This interchange, which I observed casually, is entirely consistent with the results of a set of 2008 studies of researchers' work practices. In 80 interviews at four institutions, we asked scholars how they had found out about the resources they happened to be using in their research at the time of the interview. In 28% of the cases, they had learned of these resources through personal interaction with another individual, usually a colleague, an instructor, or a student. When we add cases in which researchers had learned of the resource by tracing bibliographies and footnotes, the figure rises to 43%.[3]

An aside in Andrew Abbott's work on the meaning and value of browsing in library-based research illuminates these practices. He writes,

> Browsing has two requirements. First, the materials being browsed must already themselves be highly ordered either by virtue of their internal structure or by their places in an indexing or cataloguing or classification system. Otherwise, adjacency has no meaning and browsing can't work. Second, the browsers must have broad knowledge that primes them to recognize likely connections. This is the

rationale for general exams, for example. (Note that by this argument, one can even think of conversation with other scholars as a form of mutual browsing.) (Abbott, 2006, p. 18)[4]

Researchers, especially those who use the library as their laboratory, browse each other to find authoritative resources. They ask each other directly for useful resources and they mine each other's bibliographies and footnotes. They figure out who is doing interesting work and follow them. A good example of this comes from an interview with a bench scientist who speculated that other scientists come to his website to learn who he is and what kind of work he does. He had come to that conclusion because he used the websites of other scientists to do exactly that. He added, however, that he found himself doing this less and less. As the years go by, he explained, "I know more of the people in my field."

Researchers see their worlds as networks of people working in the same or related fields. To find information they trace through the authors to find their writings. Inexperienced researchers must learn who is who and develop their own networks. Absolute novices may have a completely opposite view, thinking of books and articles as objects lying around here and there, to be located with search engines of one kind or another.

This picture of scholarly process is corroborated in the anthropology blog *Savage Minds*. "Doing a 'literature' review, then, basically means creating a series of dossiers of the scholars with whom you will be interacting. The more creepily complete, the better." Not only will this net you the resources you need, it also, "reflects the existence of a very real network of scholars who will evaluate you on grant applications, peer review, and tenure and promotion" (Golub, 2012).

What does it take for a student to grasp this view of scholarship? To understand, first of all, that *people* write books and articles, they do not just fall from the sky. And to trace out the networks—learn who did the seminal work, who is doing related work, whose work they need to read.

It takes a few things. For one, it takes a little experience, such as exposure in a survey course, getting a few key readings under your belt, knowing a few of the more important issues and debates in a field. It also takes some maturity to put it all together and do well academically, and, in particular, it takes the maturity to recognize and engage in academia's various networks of relationship.[5] And finally, it takes an understanding of the research process as conducted by those who have done it long and well and a commitment to following that process where it may lead, rather than imposing tools on people that mystify what books, articles, and other resources really are.

The Practice of Library-Based Research

The library research process of students and faculty members has been discussed in reports on research at the University of Rochester (Foster, Clark, Tancheva, & Kilzer, 2010; Foster & Gibbons 2005; Randall, Clark, Smith, & Foster, 2008; Foster, 2009; Foster & Gibbons, 2007), as well as in the work of the sociologist Andrew Abbott (Abbott, 2008a; Abbott, 2008b; Abbott, 2008c). By library research, I refer to the process theorized by Abbott (Abbott 2008c; summarized below) that is followed by those researchers who depend primarily on the library for their informational and theoretical resources. Much of the process occurs outside of the library, but the library is essential to the process, and the way the library is used and the way it is central differentiate the library research process from the research process in the sciences, which is characterized by the generation of data in the laboratory.

Key features of the library research process include—

- *Building up a knowledge* of key works and key authors as well as an informational and theoretical base in one's discipline and especially in one's area of specialization
- *Keeping up in one's field,* however defined, through continuous scanning or browsing of new books, journals, conference schedules, abstracts, departmental talks (at one's own department and other departments that are known to be strong), and conversation with colleagues in the same and related fields
- *Developing connections to others* who share one's interests, from entering students to luminaries in the field, using a variety of means, including attending talks and conferences, corresponding or speaking in person, and otherwise participating in scholarly networks
- *Utilizing the world of sources and resources* wherever they may be and however they may be found and used, including materials in library stacks, electronic journals, archives and special collections, and "the web"—and using whatever tools could possibly work to find and get hold of these sources and resources
- *Maintaining one's own library* of resources, including print and electronic documents, books, journals, papers, notes, and correspondence, with some organizational scheme, or set of schemes, to enhance understanding on first reading and to support accretion and retrieval of information and the development and increasing complexity of one's own work
- *Producing one's own work,* incorporating one's own past work and the work of others, and then publishing or otherwise sharing manuscripts, books, reports, articles, presentations, and so on

For a researcher, using a library catalog or database represents a small portion of a large number of tactics that might be employed to get resources for specific projects and generally to keep up in one's fields. This, of course, stands in opposition to the library view in which the central position is accorded to the OPAC—the online public access catalog—and databases—electronic indexes to bodies of literature, often journal and newspaper articles. It is no surprise that library technology looks different to different people. Each of us sees the world from a personal perspective, a perspective constrained by our interests and, especially, by our responsibilities. We would expect the people who are responsible for the library's finding aids and technologies and who use them as tools in their own work to place them front and center. However, there is an explanatory benefit in seeing research from the perspective of the researcher, that is, in imagining what the world looks like to library patrons who use the OPAC and databases and all the other resources, services, and tools the library offers.[6]

Scholars conducting library research are driven by questions and engaged in a network of scholars, their works, and a variety of artifacts that inform the research pursuit. This view of library-based research and the pursuits of researchers accords people and things equivalent agency in the network of science work (Latour, 1988). Such things as journal articles and their persuasive arguments may become, for a time, at least, inarguable truths ("black boxes"), acting as authorities as much as the authors—the people—in the network act as authorities.

In interviews for the eXtensible Catalog project, we see the enormous importance given to both kinds of authority—that of respected scholars and that of classic works and discoveries.[7] Both are used as points of departure in library research, and both are used a relatively large proportion of the time, according to our studies. Indeed, authors are very much the favored nodes in our interviewees' networks; when we ask how researchers found the works they are currently using, the answer was frequently that they found them through a personal contact (a conversation with a colleague, for example), through a search for the author (already a known authority), or through a search of an authority's footnotes and bibliographies. Of course, this approach—through authors and authorities—requires a base of knowledge, one we might assume belongs only to advanced scholars. However, our research also shows that even undergraduates, when they are motivated and interested in their academic work, quickly begin to build up this kind of knowledge base, in which key authorities figure prominently. One of the surprising findings of research for eXtensible Catalog is that many of the undergraduates who are most successful at research have attended a scholarly conference where they met some key people in their field. Indeed, there is some evidence in our research that a key moment in the intellectual development of undergraduate researchers is the realization that all those books and articles are written by people, and that they might meet and talk with those people, and perhaps study with them or become their colleagues one day.

Research Support at the Desk

When an undergraduate approaches a librarian at the desk, the librarian may respond in a variety of ways, since there is no single, uniform process or method of conducting a reference interview. When I questioned librarians at the University of Rochester about their training in library school and about standard or influential models of the reference interview, they averred that there is no consistency in training or practice and that the same was true of bibliographic instruction. A limited search of the literature, conducted by two reference librarians and the author, supported this. Documents from the website of the American Library Association put forth standards of librarian behavior at the reference

desk and in the classroom (ALA Reference and User Services Association, 2004; Association of College and Research Libraries, 2001). These standards revolve mainly around helping patrons focus their questions and then using a variety of tools to locate appropriate items; they also provide guidance on such aspects of public service as being approachable, demonstrating interest, and listening attentively. These documents do not present or consider the perspective or the practices of the researcher, other than to acknowledge that the researcher comes to the librarian with a question or an assignment, which serves as the starting point for the interaction. This starting point is implicit in other sources that our search identified. For example, we found many journal articles that focus on instructional strategies and updated approaches for reaching today's students (Kennedy, Cole, & Carter, 1997; Malone & Videon, 2003; Oberg, 1999); most of this literature is practical and process oriented, sometimes presenting typologies (White, 1987) or using psychological theories to understand and reach out to students (McNeer, 1991).

An interesting approach is used by Wang, who works within a Vygotskian framework via the work of Jean Lave, to propose literacy-teaching activities based on a theory of learning in practice (Wang, 2007). Lave's work on "cognition in practice" presupposes that learning goes on everywhere, at all times, and that it is part of larger social processes whereby members of "communities of practice" move to the center (positions of expertise and leadership) from the periphery (a "legitimate" starting point for the novice; see Lave, 1988). Wang suggests that librarians might harness the dynamics of peer-to-peer and peer-to-expert groups to activate the movement from novice toward expert in the area of information literacy. While Wang's work focuses on learning, not on research, it assumes that research is a social process; it is about the social context of inside-the-head development, the psychological side of Lave.

The sociological side of Lave is also useful for understanding what research is, that is, for contributing to a theory of library research and then illuminating the empirical research and helping us apply it to library practice. If learning is movement from periphery to center in a community of practice, we could say that different students are moving toward the center of different communities of practice; indeed, one student may be involved in research that engages multiple communities of practice. For example, we interviewed a student who is interested in underwater archaeology—he is currently pursuing an advanced degree in this area—and wrote papers on a variety of topics, some central to his interests and others less compelling to him, personally. When doing research for a paper related to his area of specialization, the student already knew some of the key authors and classic texts and had a substantial informational base. He even has some standing in the community of underwater archaeologists from past projects and conference attendance and thus was able to launch his research from a substantial base. In writing this paper, the student was working toward centrality in the community of underwater archaeologists; in other classes and on other papers, he may have been working toward centrality in a community with little or no relation to his academic and vocational interests. For example, he might in other courses be engaged with a community of students at his college who are simply on track to complete their degrees or who know something about science or humanities—communities, to be sure, but ones that do little to forward this student's engagement with the literature in his or any other field.

Students, engaged in many communities, may find that their research assignments help them move toward greater centrality in those communities in which they are working, providing additional ways to build relationships and gain information. That is, depending upon the assignment, one student may be engaged and informed because of past experience and ongoing interests, while another may simply be getting the job done. This is in contrast to senior scholars who tend to occupy central positions in their fields of research *across projects.* Put another way, when a student approaches a librarian, the student might or might not be informed and interested in the assignment, but when a faculty member approaches a library about his or her own research, that faculty member is almost certain to have advanced knowledge and be densely enmeshed in the associated scholarly networks.

Published guidelines for reference service and information literacy instruction, with their focus on the clarification of questions and the use of finding aids, are best suited either for students who have little grounding in the topic and are looking for items that will help them complete an assignment or for more advanced scholars who need help finding particular resources or want to trace through the work of other authors to find previously unknown works. However, these guidelines do not speak to the way that serious scholars do their research by the process, glossed above, in which a sustained inquiry into a set of intellectual and informational problems drives the development of relations with other authors and researchers and their ideas and writings. In fact, they clash in practice and in theory, as I explain below.

Librarians Are Researchers, Too

With regard to research, we most often see librarians acting as librarians in libraries, responding to requests for research help, and we see faculty members and students, likewise, in the academic setting, working on short- or long-term projects. What would happen, we wondered, if we watched librarians, faculty members, and students do research on their own areas of academic specialization or on non-academic topics? Would they follow a similar process to each other? And would that process resemble the library research process of scholars? As far as our preliminary results go, yes and yes. Across these three groups, the process of finding information on a topic close to one's heart, for which accurate, timely, and robust information is required, the question drives the process, the researcher builds up a base of knowledge through key works (books, pamphlets, websites) and authorities (known experts, friends, fellow fans, salespeople, respected organizations), and then works these connections for more information, using whatever tools are at his or her disposal, including Google, Wikipedia, and Amazon; museum collections; local libraries; online literature; personal libraries; and the information offerings of hardware stores, sporting goods stores, garden centers, and other retail establishments.

What follows are four examples in which librarians and faculty members recounted for us how they found information in non-academic areas that are of great personal interest to them.

A librarian talks about finding literature about a certain kind of antique textile, mainly on a used book site, and using the literature to identify gaps in her collection:

> I had some books that had a bibliography in the back, and started looking that way. And then had people's last names. [Searches ABE Books for authors.]… If you look at the sources [referring, for example, to the catalog of a major collector]. These are collections that have great, big coffee table books…. So you can see the whole range of what's out there.

Another librarian describes a variety of tools she used in a process of seeking information about a health problem:

> So, running injuries. OK. And how did I come up with the name of my problem? Plantar fasciitis… I'm sure I Googled but I put in lots of words. I

read a lot of articles that talk about, I mean, the way people search they'll just put in one word or they might just put in "heel pain" and put in "heel pain running de-dah-de-dah"—I put in a bunch of words to try to get something closer to the mark. I might actually go to somewhere like a medlineplus.gov… the right way to do it!… No—all we ever do is Google…. I went to YouTube and I searched YouTube. And there are a whole bunch of videos of exercises and what to do about the problem…. My husband, he is always telling me, "Oh, YouTube has videos on how to juggle and how to do this and how to—"… Here's another one. A friend of mine from a theatre company said, "Oh, I had that problem and there's an article in Runner's World about strengthening your hips to fix your feet."… I never found that article. She had to send it to me…. I know it fixed her problem. I know she's a really dedicated runner.

A faculty member describes the process he used to do background research for a novel he is writing. Much of the action takes place in a suburb, G, of the city, M.

> I'm writing a novel set in M. I know that there's a portion of the book that is set in this suburb of G. I didn't spend a lot of time in G when I was in M, and so something that I did do [conducting Google search on name of suburb]. So I actually ended up using this [information about contact person, listed on public website] to call her. And so I called her, and I explained, "I'm writing this book. You serve in the government of G, but you work in real estate; you're in the garden club." And I was telling her about this house, this large house that I imagined things being set in, and I thought she might have some advice about what the grounds might look like, or what the garden club element might be. This led to a conversation that actually led to me then talking to somebody who led me to talk to somebody who led to somebody,

and then when I went back to M recently, I met her. She drove me around and sort of showed me some of the developments and things.

Another faculty member talks about using the local library and building a small personal collection of information to find out about local Amish and Mennonite communities:

So, I visited a Shaker museum a few years ago, and then I wanted to read about them, and then utopian societies; things like that. For that, I always go to the library and get books. I'm reading right now a little bit about Amish and Mennonite societies, just because in this part of the world, we brush shoulders fairly frequently…. Yeah, so for those—for that sort of interest, I always just go to the library and look on the shelves for books. And I've never actually ever looked it up on the Internet; I don't know why…. There's two—I would call them booklets—next to my bed, and I think they were both authored by someone named Hoffstetler, who is a member of a plain folk community, as he has described. But I read another great book from the library, and I don't remember who wrote it…. Those I own; my husband got them for me as a gift… They're used. He found them at the little antique co-op downtown because he knew I was interested, because I was reading this other book, which I had to keep checking out over and over and over because I read it so slowly, two or three pages a night.

Faculty members use similar processes whether conducting library research in their academic specialties or finding information about the things in their private lives that intrigue them. They put the question first and use libraries, personal connections, and other means to get the information they need. The building of a network of connections, with people and objects at the nodes, is quite clear as they describe

what they did to get information for a particular project or need.

Librarians have an extraordinary skill in using online catalogs, databases, and other finding aids to get the information they want for personal reasons, and they use this skill and these tools for some of their research, but only for some. Like other researchers, when pursuing their own interests, librarians put the question first and use whatever tools will work, developing a base of knowledge through the accretion of classic or reliable information sources (people and objects). The clash is not between librarians, on the one hand, and faculty members and students, on the other. It is between librarians pursuing their own research interests and librarians in the professional setting.

Understanding Research

The sociologist Andrew Abbott provides a theory of library research, writing specifically of the advanced research of scholars who rely primarily or very heavily on academic libraries and similar collections for their data, as is the case in many disciplines in the humanities and social sciences, such as history and literature (Abbott, 2008c) in contrast to more familiar systems like standard social scientific research. Contrasting library research to the "standard research" associated with science disciplines, Abbott points first to the difference in the organization of the data. While standard researchers organize their data themselves, library researchers work with complexly organized collections. Standard researchers measure their data while library researchers read and browse; in his computational framework, this means that the two use very different algorithms for finding, absorbing, and using the data. Standard research is ordered and sequential, library research partial and recursive, and so on. One of Abbott's key insights is the artisanal nature of library research and the "multitasking" it requires; again, in the computational framework, Abbott experiences his brain working at many levels, some in the forefront—such as looking for information through a variety of sources—and some in the background—assessing those sources for reliability, for example. But perhaps the most striking of Abbott's characterizations of library research is that it requires its practitioners to be "prepared"—that is, to bring to the task of library research the foundation of information, experience, and skill that is required for successful browsing and reading, searching and assessing. And as to the goals of library research, "the overall thing library researchers aim to optimize is not a 'truth' but a richness and plenitude of interpretations" (Abbott, 2008c, p. 538)in contrast to more familiar systems like standard social scientific research.

While Abbott writes from the point of view of the researcher, elucidating the scholar's process, he considers this process in its broader context. The context is another kind of network, one of people, ideas, books, articles, lab equipment, and so on. This network looks different to the various students, librarians, and faculty members who are bringing more or less richly developed neural networks to the task. The longer people work in a field, the more they know and see of this network. Those who have put in the most years—read a lot, met a lot of people, gone to conferences, and so on—see the most.

The more advanced scholars are familiar with the classic works and authors, and they know many of the active researchers in their field; hear about their projects; read their articles; and understand the connections between the various scholars, labs, departments, books and articles, reports, and so on. Accordingly, our studies at the University of Rochester, Yale University, Ohio State University, and Cornell University suggest that full-fledged researchers search for information through people. For example, many of the faculty members we studied Googled the names of people they knew, found their work on departmental webpages, and then networked from those people to others working on related problems. Faculty members and others who are accomplished researchers see big portions of research networks.

Students see a smaller portion—they see what pokes up on the small surface of what they know. They see mainly books and articles, although those with the interest and the opportunity, say, to attend a conference see some—but only some—of the larger connections.

Librarians at the University of Rochester say that when engaged in reference work, they themselves tend to have a professional view of books and articles as objects out there.[8] They use specialized tools designed to find known objects or objects related deep in their metadata or to find objects that cite or are cited by others. I argue that this professional approach to finding is at odds not only with what faculty researchers do, it is at odds with what librarians themselves do when they are doing research on something that is within their own sphere of expertise. Nonetheless, it is the approach that they use with students, and it reinforces the fundamental difference between the research practices of faculty members and the approach of many students, especially younger students or students researching topics in which they have little interest. The librarian and the student search through this imagined field of books and articles scattered about, with the game being to find the right ones in the shortest amount of time. What I would like to suggest is that this approach is excellent for a last-minute assignment, a narrowly focused search or tracking back through cited works, but that research is much more than this. And that librarians are already good at the other methods used by the serious researchers Abbott discusses because in their own areas of interest, librarians *are* serious researchers.

And Using this Understanding

Librarians can benefit from gaining empirical data about what research is so they can be more conscious of their own research processes and use that knowledge to develop tools for helping others do research, at the desk and in the classroom. If librarians saw themselves as researchers with a big bag of tricks, a good foundation of knowledge in their fields of interest, and connections to others who share those interests they would be in a better position to encourage students to develop a more mature perspective, one more closely aligned with that of their professors. And it could help librarians develop strategies that are more likely to work because they are informed by theory and based on empirical data about real researchers in real situations.

Librarians have four years to work with undergraduates in a variety of situations, from last-minute crises to sustained projects of great interest, and they have many more years to build relationships with graduate students and faculty members. With students, there are opportunities to use a theory-based approach to help students recognize, use, and build networks (Weir, 2010). With faculty members, there is a prospect of partnership in this regard, as well as opportunities to expand support from "searching" to "researching"—to the more sustained building of knowledge through library-based research and the browsing and reading and connecting it entails, researcher to researcher.

Notes

1. This chapter includes material from papers presented at the 2010 Association of Research Libraries' Library Assessment Conference, Baltimore, Maryland, and the 2012 Academic Librarians Conference, Syracuse University, Syracuse, NY.

2. See Chapter 6, "'Whatever Works': Finding Trusted Information," for information about the methods and findings of the key study reported here. Other information is drawn from user research for eXtensible Catalog, discussed in *Scholarly Practice, Participatory Design and the eXtensible Catalog* (Foster, Clark, Tancheva, & Kilzer, 2010).

3. By contrast, 19% had found their resources by searching a database, the OPAC, WorldCat, Amazon, Google, and Google Scholar combined. We also found that 25% consulted their own accrued knowledge base (including classics and other books they owned); 8% browsed stacks and special collections; and the remainder relied on handbooks, e-mail alerts, and other miscellaneous means. For more information, see "What Researchers Do: Briefs on User Research for the eXtensible Catalog" (http://hdl.handle.net/1802/12376).

4. Browsing may seem casual when compared to the more formal and structured searching for information that researchers do with a variety of indices, databases, catalogs, and other tools. However, formal and informal information gathering have much in common. The researcher begins to build a mental knowledge base by reading classic and assigned texts, for example, in college and graduate school courses (cf. the "general exams" mentioned by Abbott, above). The researcher adds to this knowledge base through a wide variety of activities, including writing papers, attending talks, joining scholarly societies, reading journals, conducting literature reviews, going to conferences, meeting people working in the same and related fields, and so on. Throughout all of these activities, researchers simultaneously engage in formal and informal information gathering, that is, in information gathering they consciously structure as a search or conduct opportunistically at any time and place. The conjunction of the structured materials and the prepared mind, Abbott's two requirements for browsing, are essential in all cases. Or, as Abbott says elsewhere, "browsing—broadly understood as the productive confrontation between an ordered, informed mind and a differently ordered set of materials—is going on at all levels of investigation at all times" (Abbott 2008a).

5. See Chapter 5, "Learning the Ropes," for information on how students mature in college.

6. See William Arms's "A Viewpoint Analysis of the Digital Library" in this regard (2005).

7. We conducted a total of 80 workplace interviews of faculty members, graduate students, and undergraduates at four institutions, focusing mainly on how they had acquired the sources and resources they were using and how they keep up in their fields. We interviewed productive scholars— established scholars who are actively publishing or students who are deemed by their professors to show promise—in all fields but mostly in the humanities and humanistic social sciences. For more information, see "XC User Research Preliminary Report" (Foster, 2009).

8. I owe this insight to Helen Anderson, head of Collection Development at the University of Rochester's River Campus Libraries; it was confirmed in subsequent conversations with many other Rochester librarians.

References

Abbott, A. (2006). *The University library.* Retrieved from http://home.uchicago.edu/aabbott/Papers/libreport.pdf

Abbott, A. (2008a, March). *Library research and its infrastructure in the twentieth century.* Paper presented at the Windsor Lecture, University of Illinois. Retrieved from http://home.uchicago.edu/~aabbott/Papers/illinois.pdf

Abbott, A. (2008b, June). *Publication and the future of knowledge.* Paper presented at the Association of American University Presses, Montreal. Retrieved from http://home.uchicago.edu/~aabbott/Papers/aaup.pdf

Abbott, A. (2008c). The traditional future: A computational theory of library research. *College and Research Libraries, 69*(6), 523–545. http://crl.acrl.org/content/69/6/524.abstract.

ALA Reference and User Services Association. (2004). Guidelines for behavioral performance of reference and information services professionals. Retrieved from http://www.ala.org/Template.cfm?Section=Home&template=/ContentManagement/ContentDisplay.cfm&ContentID=26937

Arms,W.Y. (2005, July). A viewpoint analysis of the digital library. *D-Lib Magazine, 11*(7/8). Retrieved from http://www.dlib.org/dlib/july05/arms/07arms.html

Association of College and Research Libraries. (2001). Objectives for information literacy instruction: A model statement for academic librarians Retrieved from http://www.ala.org/ala/mgrps/divs/acrl/standards/objectivesinformation.cfm

Foster, N.F., Clark, K., Tancheva, K., & Kilzer, R. (Eds.) (2010). *Scholarly Practice, Participatory Design and the eXtensible Catalog.* Retrieved from http://hdl.handle.net/1802/12375

Foster, N.F. (2009). *XC user research preliminary report.* Retrieved from UR Research website: http://hdl.handle.net/1802/687

Foster, N.F. & Gibbons, S. (2005). Understanding faculty to improve content recruitment for institutional repositories. *D-Lib Magazine, 11*(1). Retrieved from http://www.dlib.org/dlib/january05/foster/01foster.html

Foster, N.F. & Gibbons, S. (Eds.) (2007). *Studying students: The undergraduate research project at the University of Rochester.* Retrieved from UR Research website: http://hdl.handle.net/1802/7520

Golub, A. (2012). It's the people, stupid. [Web log post]. Retrieved from http://archive.feedblitz.com/42193/~4169364

Kennedy, L., Cole, C., & Carter, S. (1997). Connecting online search strategies and information needs: A user-centered, focus-labeling approach. *RQ, 36*(4), 562–568.

Latour, B. (1988). *Science in action: How to follow scientists and engineers through society.* Cambridge, MA: Harvard University Press.

Lave, J. (1988). *Cognition in practice: Mind, mathematics and culture in everyday life.* New York, NY: Cambridge University Press.

Malone, D. & Videon, C. (2003). *First year student library instruction programs.* Chicago, IL : Association of College &

Research Libraries.

McNeer, E.J. (1991). Learning theories and library instruction. *Journal of Academic Librarianship, 17*(5), 294–297.

Oberg, D. (1999, August). Teaching the research process—for discovery and personal growth. Paper presented at IFLA Council and General Conference, Bangkok, Thailand. Retrieved from http://archive.ifla.org/IV/ifla65/papers/078-119e.htm

Randall, R., Clark, K., Smith, J., & Foster, N.F. (2008). *The next generation of academics: A report on a study conducted at the University of Rochester.* Retrieved from UR Research website: http://hdl.handle.net/1802/6053

Wang, L. (2007). Sociocultural learning theories and information literacy teaching activities in higher education. *Reference & User Services Quarterly, 47*(2), 149.

Weir, R. (2010, July). Using library experts wisely. *Inside Higher Ed.* Retrieved from http://www.insidehighered.com/advice/instant_mentor/weir27

White, M.D. (1987). The reference interview: Impact of environmental constraints. Retrieved from http://www.eric.ed.gov/ERICWebPortal/contentdelivery/servlet/ERICServlet?accno=ED309784

chapter eight. Understanding How Undergraduates Work

Sarada George and Nancy Fried Foster

We called our first research project with undergraduates "Papers Happen" because we really did not know what happened between the time their professors assigned papers and students handed them in. We wanted to understand the step-by-step process by which students selected their topics; found and used resources; consulted professors, librarians, and others who might help; and reviewed and revised their papers for final submission. It seemed like a good idea to ask the students how they accomplished these tasks, but how to ask? The ethnographic methods we had developed in previous work seemed like a good way to start.

We had gained enormous insight into the scholarly work practices of our faculty members during the design of our institutional repository (Foster & Gibbons, 2005). That project, funded by the Institute for Museum and Library Services,[1] introduced work-practice study and participatory design to our library, methods we decided to apply to our new questions about undergraduate work practices (Foster & Gibbons, 2007)especially in the areas of reference outreach, online catalogs, institutional repositories, and Web-based services. Still, the library staff wanted to do more to reach students and their instructors in support of the university's educational mission. But to do more, we realized we needed to know more about today's undergraduate students— their habits, the academic work they are required to do, and their library-related needs. In particular, we were interested in how students write their research papers and what services, resources, and facilities would be

most useful to them. As Katie Clark, director of the Carlson Science and Engineering Library, remarked early in this project, "Papers happen," but we did not know how they happen. Thus, in the summer of 2004, a group of librarians and the River Campus Libraries' lead anthropologist met at a park on the shore of Lake Ontario for lunch and a discussion of some research we might do to enlarge our knowledge of undergraduate work processes. Many of us had participated in a previous study, supported by a grant from the Institute for Museum and Library Services, to examine the work practices of faculty members in order to build a better institutional repository (Foster and Gibbons 2005. Our first steps were to question instructors about their expectations of student papers and to have students reflect on a recent, completed paper, telling and showing us what they had done. Information gleaned from student maps and photographs and from inquiries into student development and information-finding strategies filled out the picture.[2]

In this chapter, we discuss the student research and writing process as we understand it from all our research with undergraduates, especially the significance in this process of maturity and an ability to reach out and connect to people and information. We begin with a discussion of our findings in the 2004–2005 study of undergraduates. We then review findings from a restudy conducted in 2011, noting some similarities and differences among students and between the earlier and later studies. We conclude by asking how we can refine or change library services or facilities as we improve our knowledge of the students' research and writing processes and their professors' expectations.

Findings from 2004–2005

When we asked faculty members in late 2004 and early 2005 to tell us the hallmarks of great student papers, we could not identify a consistent, shared set of expectations, but we did get a sense of the major issues from the instructors' point of view. In general, we found that instructors expected students to be able to write a paper that demonstrated understanding of the assignment, had an interesting topic, cited relevant and respectable resources, made a good argument, and was well written and organized (Alvarez & Dimmock, 2007, p. 4). Instructors reported problems related to the use of relevant literature. Their hope was that students would discern the relevant, reliable resources; approach those resources with a critical attitude; and relate the arguments and information in those resources to major ideas in the course. In the weaker papers, "students tend to summarize readings instead of reflecting upon them and writing critical, thoughtful papers" (Alvarez & Dimmock, 2007, p. 5).

Once we had developed a sense of faculty expectations, we turned to the students themselves, conducting interviews with 14 of them (see Appendix 8A for the interview protocol). We asked them to draw comic-strip pictures in a rough flow chart, while telling the story of their

work on a recent research paper.[3] These "retrospective interviews" provided us with our first insights into the overall paper-writing process: Students were working on their papers late into the night; they were using online resources from remote locations; they were consulting others— most surprisingly their parents—while writing their papers.

While the retrospective interviews did not tell us everything we needed to know about how students wrote their papers, they did provide us with a sense of the overall process, an indication of how much the process might vary from student to student, and a number of questions to ask next. Subsequent photo interviews, dorm visits, and observations provided additional insight on student schedules, activities in the library, work practices in private spaces and at night, the technologies students used, and how academic work fit into life in general.

Four Students

When we reviewed the first group of retrospective interviews and the associated maps, photographs, and observations, we were struck by the range of student experience and realized that any attempt to develop a single model of the student research and writing process would not be supported by the data. Instead, we developed descriptions of four representative students, which let us establish the variability of their

Figure 8.1. Detail of a drawing produced by a student in the course of a retrospective interview

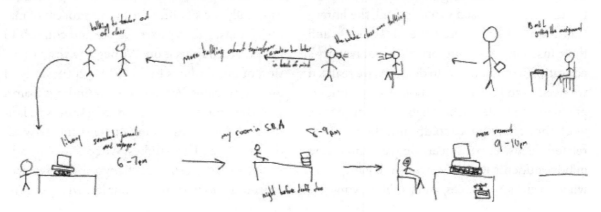

approach to college as the context of the list of generic steps we identified across research and writing processes. The following paragraphs provide snapshots of these real students.

Abbie

Abbie[4] was a driven and diligent student with exceptional organizational and writing skills. She scheduled her academic tasks on her calendar and was always up to date in her work. Abbie made regular use of the library, frequently consulting reference librarians, and had a weekly standing appointment with a tutor at the college writing center, even though she was already an excellent writer. She took advantage of a wide range of college resources and had found funding for travel to student conferences in distant locations. She kept in touch with students she met through travel and networked with them for information on topics related to her coursework and her career plans.

Danielle

Danielle developed a strong career interest about halfway through college, but even before she did, she had already demonstrated a hearty appetite for learning. Delighting in the search for office supplies and in browsing through the library's stacks, Danielle loved being in college, that is, being here now, in a physical world. While not a straight-A student, Danielle was on the dean's list most semesters and aimed to do well enough to gain admission to a professional school. Danielle approached her academic work with the same here-and-now orientation she had to the rest of her life; indeed, her academic work seemed fully integrated into life in general, and likewise an opportunity for experimentation and enjoyment.

Tiffany

Tiffany barely maintained a passing GPA in her first couple of years at college and avoided the library, staying away from both the building and the website. She seemed much more connected to her paid work, late-night shifts on a blue-collar job with no connection at all to her studies, and had little interest in her courses, no particular approach to writing papers and no evident engagement in her own education. Almost by accident, Tiffany signed up for a course completely different from her intended major. This course, like a thunderclap, captured Tiffany's interest, engaged her gifts, and transformed her into a passionate student. Her new field was extremely practical and work-oriented rather than theoretical. Tiffany became an interested, connected student who achieved success in her own practical way.

Brandon

Brandon was intelligent and resourceful; he found numerous activities in college to occupy his time and many friends with similar interests. What eluded Brandon was a major that really sang to him or any viable idea about what to do with the rest of his life. Consequently, he seemed on the surface to perform well academically but, at the end, was left wondering what the four years had been about. He never wanted to enter the library building, although he was easily able to find and use online resources. For Brandon, consulting an expert would mean asking a friend; he said he never asked a librarian a question and made no mention of engaging with faculty members or other scholars.

Steps in the Paper-Writing Process

The steps that follow appeared frequently in the stories students told about doing their papers:

- Reviewing the requirements, which might involve consulting with the instructor
- Talking over the preliminaries with others, such as a TA, librarian, or even a parent
- Attending an optional or required bibliographic instruction session
- Choosing a topic, perhaps through consultation of preliminary resources

- Creating a plan for completing the assignment
- Finding books, articles, and other resources
- Creating an outline for the paper
- Completing required assignments related to paper writing, such as submitting a topic statement for approval or creating an annotated bibliography
- Consulting with an expert, such as the course instructor or TA, a writing tutor, or a librarian
- Writing, almost always an idiosyncratic process of free-form or outline-driven composition done during or after research, over the course of weeks or months (but often in one stretch, which may be on the night before the paper is due)
- Getting feedback on the draft from peers, parents, a writing tutor, or others
- Revising the paper, often entailing a search for additional resources
- Completing the formatting and the bibliography, perhaps with the aid of an electronic bibliographic tool
- Submitting the final work on paper or electronically

We list these steps that appeared in drawing after drawing, but we do not suggest that all students followed the same pathway through them, or even that all students followed all of the steps. Rather, we find that students demonstrate a great degree of variability in how they approach their work; how strongly they demonstrate interest and commitment to reading, writing, and understanding; how and to what degree they connect themselves to their field's authorities, such as their instructors, peers, librarians, authors, or other experts; how they choose and use tools, from paper and pencil to digital technologies; and much, much more.

Timelines and Schedules

Many of the students we interviewed seemed to work on their papers in intensive spurts, especially toward the end when they were doing the actual writing. They described these bouts of work as responses to deadlines in the syllabus for choosing a topic and then turning in a bibliography, a first draft, or the final paper. Only a few students began to write the paper early in the semester, most waiting until immediately before it was due. Many told us that they had worked in spurts even when writing early drafts. For example, one freshman in our first set of interviews said, "Writing the rough draft? I think what I did was I just like sat down and locked myself in my room for two straight days and just wrote it."

Apart from work they did in class at the professor's direction, or just after a class in which the assignment was discussed, students seemed to do most of the real work on their papers in the evening or late at night, after library staff had gone home. This was confirmed by interviews we conducted late at night in dorm rooms in conjunction with our first set of retrospective interviews. The majority of students we interviewed in both of these sub-projects appeared to be "night owl" workers (Bell & Unsworth, 2007).

Using the Library and Finding Resources

The undergraduates we interviewed in 2005 seemed to focus primarily on online resources; they wanted to find articles in full text and e-mail them to themselves or print them. Some students told us that they had been exposed to one or more library databases in high school and brought that familiarity with them to the university. They tended to gravitate toward those familiar databases exclusively, however, and were less likely to try out new, unfamiliar databases unless the professor or someone similar mentioned them specifically and recommended them. They often started their research with Google or a similar search engine. That does not mean they ended there—they did go beyond basic search engines—but several of them told us that what they could find online was all the information there was, that is, if they could not find information on a particular topic, it simply did not exist.

Librarians think of resources according to their efficiency for particular types of tasks, but the students we spoke to tended to have a current need in mind. They lumped together all the resources they were aware of that could be used to meet that need, without regard to efficiency for the purpose. For example, if the library catalog and an aggregator database both allowed access to full-text journal articles, students rarely saw a difference between them and could be unaware that not everything listed in the database would be available in our library. In general, they had trouble distinguishing which resources were available on campus and which were not. In spite of this confusion, however, they were confident that they could find what they needed on their own.

The students we interviewed used the library primarily as a place to study or even to escape from the distractions of other locations. They seemed to do a great deal of work on papers from their dorm rooms—not just the writing, but the research as well. They would go online and expect to be able to find, read, print, or annotate all the articles required for their papers.

In spite of the availability of many resources online, many students still printed articles and some even took notes with paper and pen, though there were others more oriented to computers. The students tended to use computers frequently but usually did not carry laptops around campus. More than one student mentioned that their laptops were heavy and they did not want to tote them around all day.

Getting Help from Others

In their approach to paper writing, we observed that students tended to see the professor in the course as the primary or sole authority on the entire process. If the professor suggested using specific journals or databases or mentioned the name of a particular subject librarian, some of the students would consult those resources. If he or she made no such particular recommendation, students were much less likely to think independently of using library resources or consulting library staff. Librarians and library staff were seen as the people to ask if a student could not find a particular volume on the shelf, but not as the ones who could help them discover the best books and articles for their research. They had little idea of what librarians and library staff could do for them.

While students seemed to appreciate bibliographic instruction when it was presented to them in class, they did not seek it out. They rarely approached the reference desk to ask for help unless they happened to recognize the librarian at the desk from a previous class presentation. Instead, they felt they could find everything they needed independently, without missing anything important. They were not disabused of this notion by the results of their work; in general, they were satisfied with the grades they received for their papers, and when asked if they would do anything differently the next time, most said no, although they sometimes expressed a desire to get started earlier. In particular, we noted that they did not mention consulting a librarian the next time or using library resources more fully.

They did ask others for help, however. Most were aware of the existence of the College Writing Center and some had used or planned to use it. This was likely influenced by the fact that many of the students we interviewed in 2005 were enrolled in writing-intensive courses, either in the required introductory writing class or in upper-level courses with an additional component to satisfy the writing requirement for graduation. Others asked for help from family and friends, especially in choosing a paper topic or copy-editing their writing before they finished and handed in the final version. A number of students mentioned e-mailing a paper draft home for a parent to read and comment on before it was turned in. The fact that many of the students we interviewed in 2005 were underclassmen may have played a role here. In addition to the instances in which students reached out for help on their own, they were sometimes required by the course instructor to participate in an in-class peer review process.

At the time, we were surprised at the extent to which students consulted their parents. We realized that they looked to their instructors for the final word on requirements, perhaps because these requirements were not consistent from instructor to instructor and students knew they needed clarity. We were surprised, however, that students had so little interaction with librarians when they needed help finding resources, asking their professors and instructors instead, if indeed they sought help at all. We were also left wondering about the process by which students "grew up" academically, since we perceived from many of their stories that time and maturity were essential to their success as students.

The Restudy in 2011

Within a few years of our first study, we began to realize that some of the student work practices we observed from 2005 to 2007 had changed again, as had a number of the tools that students, faculty members, and librarians used in their academic work. For example, the use of BlackBoard and online reserves grew considerably; Apple computers, especially MacBooks, became much more popular; larger numbers of students had smart phones with data plans; our university made a significant increase in the size of its undergraduate student body; and in many ways, large and small, we saw our institution, our library, and our students changing. Within a few years we knew that we wanted to study our students all over again.

In 2011, we decided to repeat many of the same activities from the first Undergraduate Research Project to see what was the same, what had changed, and how the library could make additional adjustments to provide students with better resources and services. We conducted retrospective interviews with another 10 students and found that students seemed to rely less on their peers and their parents but much more on online resources. Surprisingly, many of them were heavy users of paper and pen for scheduling, notes, and even communication. But more importantly, we found a greater spread between those students who cared little for their assignment and worked only hard enough to get an acceptable grade and others who showed enormous passion for their topics, built their papers on an extensive foundation of information, and spoke of their professors as if they were colleagues rather than professors and instructors.

Three Students

Here are brief snapshots of three students we interviewed in 2011. Those described here are good representatives of the range of 10 students we interviewed, regarding engagement with the material, interest in the assignment, and the extent of their commitment to doing a good and thorough job. The first student, Tanya, did not lead us to believe that the paper was very important or significant or that the instructor had high expectations for what she submitted. Mandi, a younger student, seemed to have a deep and abiding interest in the subject matter but suggested that the paper was one of a multitude of assignments she had to juggle in her freshman year. The third student, Lee, had true passion for his topic and was deeply committed to working with his instructor toward a superior outcome. The following snapshots reveal this range and serve to illustrate the points we make later in this chapter.

Tanya

A senior majoring in a social science field, Tanya wrote a three-page paper about a major political figure of the Civil Rights era. She learned of the assignment on the first day of class and had three weeks to complete it. On that first day, a Tuesday, Tanya chose the subject of her paper from among the names on a list supplied by the instructor. The following Sunday, she searched the library's online catalog, finding some promising titles and texting the call numbers to her phone; she then found those books in the stacks, taking a couple of others that were nearby on the shelves. She took five books home and "put them on the floor in front of my couch, and yeah, that was it. They just sat there so that I can see them, so that will remind me to look at them. But I didn't read them."

A week before the paper was due, Tanya "looked up some stuff on Google to see, just to get a synopsis, you know, some basic stuff that is all over the place." She typed the politician's name into the Google search box and browsed Wikipedia, About.com, the National Women's Hall of Fame, and a few other websites. Tanya explains, "I wanted to see just if there was any cohesion with what I found online. And if it would relate to what I had read in the books, even though I hadn't read yet, but I just wanted to see what I could find online, just like the easy stuff, before I had to read the whole books."

Tanya did not do an extensive online search because her instructor had said that online resources would not be acceptable; Tanya took this prohibition to include article databases and although much of the information on the websites was conflicting or "sketchy," some of it was borne out when she began to read the books. Of the five books Tanya found, two that had been written by her subject and a third, a biography, turned out to be useful. Tanya read one of the books in its entirety, "but it took me two days and I was running out of time. The bi-ography I read cover to cover because it was like a kid's book, but not really, like it had pictures in it, but it wasn't really—it wasn't very wordy, but it wasn't short. Like with big words. It was really easy to read, so I was able to read that one cover to cover."

As Tanya read, she took notes on the points she thought would be "valid," and she included page numbers, which she knew she would need when she wrote the paper, a task she started at 11:00 p.m. the night before it was due and finished around 8:00 a.m. Tanya slept for an hour, then quickly stopped by her workplace to print her paper. She handed it to her instructor in class at 11:00 a.m. She told us that she had done well on the paper; she was satisfied with her work.

Mandi

Mandi was a freshman when we interviewed her and she told us about writing a paper for a humanities course that was closely related to her prospective major. She learned on the first day of class that she would have to write the paper and did nothing about it until a month and a half later, when she had to select a topic. "So what I did was I went to Wikipedia and put in all of the [topics] I thought were cool, basing it off of what we talked about in class and what I knew from basic knowledge, and I was looking for something that I thought was interesting," she explained. Her basic knowledge was extensive. "When I was a kid, we moved around a lot, so it was irritating to keep on remaking new friends, so I just went to the library and read books."

After selecting her topic and having it approved by the instructor, Mandi went looking for books in the library's online catalog using some simple search terms. This netted her several books; she took them back to her dorm room and spread them out around her on the floor, where she read comfortably, leaning against her backrest. But she was "irritated" and "disappointed" because the books all seemed to restate information drawn from the same sources. At this point, Mandi turned to Google but this led her again to restatements of the same original sources. Some suggestions from her instructor did not help but all of her searching finally gave her a good idea: She realized that she could limit her search by publication date and this provided the breakthrough she needed. Mandi returned to the library and found the books that adequately, if not precisely, addressed her paper topic.

As a freshman, Mandi was juggling assignments and exams in all of her courses, and she put off work on this paper until she had completed an essay for another class. Then, "it was just before Thanksgiving. So me and my friends were all sitting in the lounge, so I'm like, 'I've got a bunch of books,' so I took them, laid them all out, and started 'Post-It-ing' them for important information…. Yeah, we were all doing work. We were having a work day because we needed one, so that's all I had to do, so I'm like, 'This is a perfectly good time,' so it was in the [dorm] lounge, which is right next to my room, go to my room, bring a stack of these big books over, and start searching for actually relevant information…. Then I had a bunch of books that didn't have any Post-Its or had very few and I put them back into the library, and I had a bunch of books that had a lot of Post-Its and I was all excited because I could use them. And then I waited until the day before it was due to write it."

On that day, Mandi spent eight hours straight working on her paper, listening to classic rock on her headphones. She worked in a friend's dorm room, "Yeah, because when I'm doing an essay, I type it up, I get a few paragraphs done, and then I take a break, and then I do more typing. Occasionally, such as the day before it's due, one of my friends would be like, 'You should do your essay,' and I'll be like, 'I should do my essay,' so it'll actually help motivate me to do my essay. So I actually kind of find it useful to have my friends nearby when I'm doing essays."

One thing Mandi never did was find articles that were closely relevant to her topic. This is because the only database she had ever learned to use was JSTOR and the articles she found there were only tangentially related to her paper. Subsequently, Mandi took a course that included bibliographic instruction and learned about many databases that would have yielded better results. She did well on the original paper though, making do with the materials she found.

Lee
Lee was a junior majoring in biology when we interviewed him; he is in graduate school now. "I tend to be a jack of all trades," he told us. "I pursue my own interests…. I love JSTOR. I'm supposed to be a biologist, but I love looking at the other disciplines." Lee had decided to take an independent study to do research on a medieval character that had already captured his interest. He had used the character's name as his IM screen name because he was attracted to his qualities and characteristics. He thought that his junior year would be the best time for a project of this type as he would be able to concentrate on it. In anticipation of the independent study, Lee met with his professor at the end of his sophomore year and together they searched the library catalog to find resources. Lee took some library books home with him during the summer and began his reading.

He talked about his process: "I take notes on the computer…. What I did first was I documented the indices of each book, looking at their references and seeing which one of those I would be interested in. I went online and checked what articles I could find, and just kind of scan it; if I thought it was relevant, I'd actually read it in detail and then I would actually take notes … I didn't actually start writing until I got back to school."

As Lee worked on his project, he became familiar with the authors and translators whose works he used. These ranged from medieval texts to exegeses and criticism and included a doctoral dissertation from the 1940s. Many of his sources were rare and he depended on his instructor to help him find some of the more esoteric items. But Lee also looked for books and articles on his own, using several databases and Google Scholar. He also went "stacks-diving … You've been down there, you know what I'm talking about. When you go in at night, the shadows are cast by this—it's kind of intimidating, but at the same time, it feels like you're journeying into forbidden knowledge, arcane things." Lee quickly learned his way around the parts of the stacks that contained relevant material. He explained that the author of the original text was "in a section all on its own, and then there would be about two shelves, about the middle-ish of my height, in which there's a lot of stuff."

Having found and digested many books and articles, Lee began to write down ideas and some paragraphs and sections of his paper. Soon he had enough material to share with the professor; they met regularly to review these drafts and bounce ideas around. He completed his paper on time but continued to work on it after the semester ended so that it could be published on a scholarly website devoted to literature of the same period. Lee was intensely engaged in the research and writing process and commented: "I don't understand why people say writing is boring, because I guess when you find something you really like, it's not."

Student Work Practices in 2011

Our undergraduates negotiate the steps from assignment to research paper in a variety of ways. A few plan and start well ahead of time, working from an impressive knowledge base, while others know or care little about the topic and throw something together at the last minute. What all students have in common is that they find a way to connect to "experts" of one kind or

another, whether in person or through books, other media, or Internet connections. Experts may be instructors, major authors or researchers in the field, and other individuals who are recognized authorities, or students may feel that they have found an expert in a reference book or on a website or Wikipedia. The degree to which students can evaluate this expertise is variable and depends on their background—how much they have read, how many different sources they have consulted, and relevant information they have already learned elsewhere. But whether students exercise good judgment or not, they do seek expertise to the extent that their skills and experience allow. Accordingly, we see a marked progression from first-year students, many of whom find it difficult to scope out a topic and find a good question or reliable information, to advanced students, who have already developed a solid informational basis, a knowledge of relevant and trusted sources and a personal, intellectual attachment to the topic.

Our 2011 interviews revealed student work processes as varied as those of 2005, and they included the same steps. Additional features of the process came into focus in the 2011 interviews, such as a more pronounced interest among several students in doing at least some of their writing with paper and pen alongside computers

Figure 8.2. A student indicates a preference for a fine pen

and other electronic devices. It seems that some students view their academic activities as a sort of craftwork and they are intentional about their choice of tools. Some showed us preferred tools, including a fine fountain pen and a leather-bound notebook.

Getting ready to work seemed extremely important to most of our interviewed students. This means that they carefully chose a time, a location, and tools for academic work that helped them concentrate and, importantly, feel connected to the big ideas and achievements in their discipline and a *habitus* of scholarship. Many students found this certain something in the library; they came to the library when they needed to do serious work, even when they did not use the physical collections. That is, while they may have gone digital with regard to information sources, students still showed profound attachments to the physical spaces that support their intellectual activity. Accordingly, in a related study of our science library (see Chapter 9), we questioned students about the advisability of removing the books to make more space for tables. They were aghast, expressing the belief that the library would no longer be a library, would no longer be a place of inspiration and calm concentration and studiousness.

Students found books, articles, and other scholarly resources in a number of ways, first and foremost through consultation with their

instructors or a librarian (see Table 8.1). Students also consulted friends and fellow students, just as established scholars consult their colleagues. Some advanced students consulted known scholars.

We are surprised that more students mentioned consulting librarians than their instructors, and with greater satisfaction. Indeed, this seems to us like a significant change from 2005 (see Table 8.2).

Table 8.2. People with whom students consulted according to 2005's retrospective interviews

Person Consulted	Total Number of Students Who Consulted Person at Left
Instructor/ Professor	7
Parent(s)	5
Friend	4
Librarian	3
Writing Fellow	2
TA	2

When they searched for resources on their own, most browsed the physical collections or used the databases to which the library subscribes (for example, JSTOR or PubMed; see Tables 8.3 and 8.4). They may also have used Google or the library's online catalog. As we learned in our 2011 interviews with faculty members about their expectations for student research papers, resources

Table 8.1. People with whom students consulted according to 2011's retrospective interviews

Person Consulted	Total Number of Students Who Consulted Person at Left	Degree of Satisfaction		
		Satisfied	Not Satisfied	Not Reported
Librarian	5	4		1
Instructor/ Professor	4	3	1	
Friend	4	3		1
Internship supervisor	1	1		
Fellow students	1	1		
Father	1	1		
Writing Fellow	1			1

Table 8.3. Sources of literature for research papers reported in 2011's retrospective interviews (includes only most frequently mentioned sources)

How student learned of or acquired resources	Number of times this method or source was used	Number of students who used this method or source
All databases mentioned	10	8
Browsing the shelves	10	4
Google	7	4
Voyager	5	4
"Library website"	4	3
Google Scholar	4	3
From professor or instructor	3	3

Table 8.4. Detail of "All databases" line in Table 8.3

How student learned of or acquired resources	Number of times this method or source was used	Number of students who used this method or source
All databases	10	8
Economics database	1	1
Medical anthropology database	1	1
PubMed	2	1
JSTOR	4	3
MLA	1	1
Unspecified database	1	1

themselves do not generally make or break a paper. Rather, it is the way students use those resources, whether they understand them and integrate them into their own argument, that makes the difference (see Chapter 2, "Hallmarks of a Good Paper").

When it came to choosing a topic, students discussed a number of practices. Some indicated that their professors had given the class a list of topics from which everyone had to choose. Those students tended to select the topic of greatest interest to them or, if there were limits on how many students could pick a particular topic, a topic that had not yet been chosen. For other students, the decision on a topic was more open-ended. One of the students we interviewed was doing an internship on a semester abroad and chose a topic that would be easy to research at the agency with which she was interning. It was still a time-consuming process to pick a topic narrow enough for her paper and she had to remind herself periodically to get going on it:

"I mean, it was also in the back of my brain, 'You need to pick a paper topic soon.'"

Another student's class was taken to the music library by the professor for a session on library research. The student told us that "at this point, when coming to this library, we had to have sort of a kind of a general idea of what we would be doing." The topic ended up being on a composer the professor had mentioned in class but though the choice interested the student somewhat, "Really, it was to get teachers off my back."

Some students picked topics on which they had some prior knowledge. One student consulted review articles to refine a topic, and several others did web searches to see whether there was enough information to write a paper on their proposed topic. One particularly mentioned wanting to know whether or not there was sufficiently interesting information to justify choosing the topic. The level of interest in the topic seems to be a determining factor whenever possible. Even when selecting from a list, students preferred the topics that interested them most. While this seems obvious, the apparent connection between the level of interest and the quality of the resulting paper is intriguing. One student who wrote a good paper despite some lack of interest in the topic mentioned having especially good paper writing skills and being good at the "mechanics" of paper writing.

Student-to-Student and Year-to-Year Variation

In 2011, as in 2005, students followed a fairly similar set of steps to complete their papers but we saw significant differences from one student to another—especially in their degree of engagement—as well as shifts from the 2005 group to the 2011 group, mainly in the area of technology.

Technology
Mobile Devices
More students carried laptops around with them in 2011 than earlier. This may be a result of greater availability of lighter, smaller, less-expensive laptops and of other mobile devices with Internet connectivity, such as smart phones and tablets on which students can read. A number of students, somewhat more than in 2005, did everything digitally, perhaps due to the proliferation of easily portable electronic communication devices.

University Technology
Another technological change for our second set of interviewees was the adoption by the University of the Blackboard course management system, which made direct connection to many online library resources and reserve materials easier than when we conducted our first interviews. In the 2005–2006 academic year, the University of Rochester used Web CT and only a few dozen courses were in the system. By the

time we conducted the second set of retrospective interviews during the 2011–2012 academic year, the University had switched to Blackboard and the number of courses included had risen to more than 1,300.

Google
Several of the students interviewed in 2011 used Google Scholar, while those interviewed in 2005 relied primarily on Google's main interface. In general, it is much easier to acquire online resources now than it was then and this shows. The later students could, for example, gain access to library databases from home more easily and reliably than the earlier students, since this no longer required specialized software but rather a general Net ID assigned to each undergraduate on matriculation.

Finding Resources
When we conducted interviews with faculty members to understand their expectations of students, we found a pervasive assumption that someone other than themselves should already have taught students how to do library research by the time they reached their junior and senior years.[5] Professors expected students to be able to use the basic resources of an academic library, even though many seemed reluctant to provide class time for librarians to provide such instruction. One professor, who was previously unaware of the possibility of in-class library instruction, was very enthusiastic when it was brought up in our interview but still did not contact the subject librarian, even after the service was suggested. Another felt that student papers would undoubtedly be better if students received help from a subject librarian but did not want to give up class time for bibliographic instruction. "There's barely enough time to cover everything as it is," he said. Time constraints were the primary reason for not scheduling in-class bibliographic instruction, but some professors also felt that

learning how to use library resources was the responsibility of the student. Further, while professors expect graduate students to become familiar with the best resources in their fields, few could articulate how their undergraduate students on track for graduate school would develop this familiarity and the research skills that go with it.

Without specific library instruction, students are left with major misconceptions of what they can find at the library or online. One student declared that "what I thought and what I still think is that the articles that they have here are catalogued on the Internet," meaning that if she cannot find an item on the web, she cannot get access to it from the library. Few students seemed familiar with interlibrary loan and some had only an elementary knowledge of the online public access catalog. Beyond this, at least one could not differentiate between the journal literature to which she had access through subscription databases and the general information she found in online searches. Since her professor had specifically disallowed the use of "online resources," this student's misunderstanding led to her belief that she could only use monographs and not journal articles in researching her paper.

The students we interviewed, both in 2005 and in 2011, relied heavily on information obtained from non-library online sources or from someone they knew personally, and, as noted above, few had the skills to evaluate either their sources or the resulting information. Their top priority usually seemed to be to get the paper written and turned in for a good grade. Their professors, on the other hand, expected that students—at least upper-level students—would evaluate sources and conduct careful, critical research for their papers.

Studying in the Library

A pattern became evident in our 2011 interviews that had not been noticeable earlier. Students tended to work together with their friends, though not necessarily on the same assignments or even for the same classes. For example, several mentioned that their friends encouraged them to get on with their work or that group study enabled them to take breaks from time to time. This was corroborated in our map and photo interviews (see Chapter 4).

Except when focused on the actual writing, usually before a looming deadline, there was a rather fuzzy boundary between work time and study breaks. A student might work alongside friends and then stop to talk, use YouTube, or text someone—or get a cup of coffee. A group of students at the same table could be doing a variety of tasks simultaneously. In observations conducted around the same time as the interviews, we found large numbers of students moving quickly among academic and non-academic activities. We also found many students working in groups, although in many cases these students did not seem to be working as much together as simply sitting next to each other.

At the same time that students appeared to be so strongly attached to their peer groups when working in the library, they reported far fewer instances of reaching out to their parents for help on their papers. As in 2005, students regarded the professor as the primary authority on both the topic of their paper and the manner of writing a paper (see Table 8.2). They also consulted a writing fellow, teaching assistants, or other graduate students associated with a professor; an internship supervisor; classmates; and, in a surprisingly large number of cases, librarians, but fewer family members.

Hanging onto Print

Though we saw a clear migration from paper to electronic resources during the interval between 2005 and 2011, for example, in the move toward more online reserves, many of the students we interviewed in 2011 still used print for reading

Figure 8.3. Items a student used for writing

articles, taking notes, or keeping track of their schedules. This was also clear in our photographic study, in which students took photos of places they studied, things they carried around, and so on. These photos frequently included pens, pencils, notebooks, assignment books, and memo books.

Some students took digital notes but others highlighted text in books and printed papers, made notes in notebooks or on other paper, or used sticky notes to mark pages containing information of interest. One student even decided which books to keep for the full loan and which to return to the library on the basis of the number of Post-It notes sticking up out of their pages.

Further Comparisons between Older and Newer Interviews

In both the first and second set of interviews, the amount of effort students put into writing their papers seemed to be directly related to their degree of interest in the subject matter and their engagement with the topic in general. The highly motivated biology major "Lee" did an independent study project on a humanities

topic of great personal interest to him and delved deeply into the literature in the field. He took library books home over the summer and then met regularly with his supervising professor during the academic year. In researching his topic, he not only used library databases to find articles but also checked the index of each book he used to find relevant search terms as well as sections of interest in the book.

Lee's interest and engagement were such that he had a favorite study area in the library and spent time browsing the shelves in the areas that deal with his general topic. He had no particular interest in library systems or librarians; he "guessed" that call numbers involved the subjects of the materials and when he asked the "nice old ladies" at the reference desk for help, it was to locate materials he already knew about. What interested Lee was the paper and the research; he took a systematic approach and did not do it all at once just before it was due, in contrast with students working on papers of lesser interest to them.

"Mandi" was one of these latter students and her snapshot reveals someone who, though working on a paper close to her interests, had limited investment in it due to other aspects of her academic situation. A freshman, Mandi had a wide range of novel tasks to accomplish; she was already doing well in the course and felt she could easily coast. She approached her professor for help but did not persist when that help was less than ideal. Reflecting on the experience some time later, Mandi realized that she could have found much more research on her topic, but that she had not yet learned how to connect to it.

Even further along the continuum, "Tanya" wrote her paper the night before it was due, even though she had known about the paper requirement from the first meeting of the class. A senior writing on a topic very close to her major interest, Tanya showed little commitment to her work and little intrinsic interest in learning about the important public figure she was researching. Compared to Lee and even Mandi, Tanya showed a decided lack of interest and engagement.

A very similar range was evident in our 2005 interviews. One student, who wrote a senior honors thesis in a social science field, revealed a high level of interest and commitment in his interview with us. He began his research enthusiastically during a summer internship, frequently using a large public library. He met with his thesis advisor regularly and submitted numerous drafts of his paper. He telephoned political groups for information and worked with a grad student on statistical analysis. In spite of his hard work, he was surprised when the professor expected him to spend even more time—some of spring break—on his thesis and to determine independently the variables he was testing. But he did the added work, even though he found it onerous and had to sacrifice other important activities to complete it. Though he did well on the thesis, he reflected that it was "a much bigger process than I had ever imagined." His interest and willingness had been tested and he had prevailed.

Speaking of the degree to which her engagement was crucial to her success at writing papers, another student in our earlier interviews discussed how she developed both skill and enjoyment of research and writing. She spoke of this in the language of paper-writing mechanics: She had "[developed] better study techniques, using more resources—for example the reference desk—just working harder in general and caring more." Her approach, far from merely mechanical, was marked by "caring more." In researching her paper, she used a few databases she found on the library's webpage and then "asked some friends from other schools and the people at the reference desk what other databases I should look at." She followed her TA's advice, explaining, "I was rather surprised to hear that he said you should spend at least 40–50% of the time doing research and planning. I thought of that and kept

that in my head and that's what I did and I think that's why I could write good papers."

It is our students' varying degrees of commitment and interest that strike us as most significant, outweighing the differences we note in digital and communication tools or how students used library buildings and other spaces. Whether in 2005 or in 2011, the students who found their academic work most compelling were the ones who talked about finding numerous resources, reading widely, and completing papers they felt were strong. In the end, we are struck by the emergence of academic connection and commitment as important themes when we review our students' narrations and drawings of their paper writing process.

Academic Connection and Commitment

As mentioned above, after we had completed our original study, we wondered about the development of students over the four years of college from callow youths to relatively engaged young adults who "know the ropes." We also wanted to know what students, their instructors and librarians do when they need reliable information on a topic that is very important to them, whether it is "academic" or not. As part of our 2011 restudy, we conducted studies in these areas (see Chapters 6, "'Whatever Works': Finding Trusted Information" and 7, "Research as Connection").

Across all of the retrospective interviews, we found that the most successful students find the work of experts, have a strong interest in the subject matter, and display overall maturity. This accords with what we learned about our students' academic development in our study of how students "learn the ropes." We spoke with undergraduates, RAs, and pre-major and major advisors to identify the moments and processes by which young people, many of whom seem "clueless" when they arrive on campus, become competent college students by the time they graduate. Our findings provide insight into the interplay of a number of intertwined developmental processes. We found it particularly helpful to see and hear, in conversations with students, faculty, and staff, how the process of becoming academically mature and competent depends on physical, social, and emotional development.

Our data fell into four descriptive categories:

1. Physical maturity: managing personal physical and health needs, such as getting enough sleep, managing stress, and, in some cases, treatment for chronic illness

2. Emotional maturity: managing academic and non-academic relationships, achieving self-awareness of personality and life circumstances

3. Social maturity: developing skill and ease in dealing with procedural demands of campus and college life, such as finding good places to study and managing time

4. Academic maturity: developing a sustained academic focus along with academic skills essential to the college environment

In brief, we learned that the process of learning the ropes is one of maturation in distinct but interrelated and mutually reinforcing ways. Students who describe themselves or are described by advisors or professors as successful or competent have made significant strides in all four categories. Importantly, academic proficiency is necessary but not sufficient for academic success. Students who arrive at college with outstanding academic skills and interests still need to develop physically, emotionally, and socially in order to excel, especially as they move from college into graduate study or the world of work. As they become mature, they seem to connect to their instructors and, especially within their majors, develop a genuine interest in their coursework. Some students become even more connected within their chosen field of study, perhaps working directly with a professor on a project; attending a conference; and coming to understand that the books, articles, and other resources they consult are written by authors who work within a dense network of scholars extending through time and space. For example, Lee spoke of his instructor as if he were a colleague and rattled off the names of the key authors in his field in a way that suggested that he saw himself as part of a bigger scholarly conversation about his topic.

This picture of students as more or less connected to the experts in their chosen fields, and more or less immersed in the literature and the debates, emerged even more strongly in another study that came out of our original undergraduate research. We investigated how students, faculty members, and librarians go about finding information on a topic that is of great personal interest and importance to them, whether or not the topic is scholarly (see Chapter 6). We conducted that study because we wanted to see how people get information when they have the strongest possible motivation to do so.

We found, among other things, that everyone has a passion for something, although not necessarily for the paper they are writing at the moment. Any student seeking information on a topic of great personal interest knows something about how to get information. We found that students, librarians, and faculty members use a similar "whatever works" process to find information across the board for scholarly and recreational topics. People, especially those who are perceived to be experts, are extremely important in the information-seeking process as seekers move from node to node through information networks in physical and virtual spaces.

The paper-writing processes followed by Abbie, Mandi, and Lee differed greatly in the extent to which each student was personally interested in the research topic and engaged with experts in the field, whether through literature or person-to-person interactions. While Abbie and Mandi were interested in their topics, it was Lee who demonstrated a much stronger drive to engage with the material to satisfy his own, very strong curiosity. Abbie and Lee had the mechanics—they had both developed good library skills—and Mandi improvised in a way that met her immediate needs, but these academic skills, while necessary, are not sufficient for the highest quality work. All three students "did well"—they got good grades on their papers. What propelled Lee to do such an outstanding job was the combination of mechanics, personal drive, connection to other experts and scholars, and the maturity to give his work the time it needed, even though that meant working over breaks. Publication of his paper on a specialist website truly brought Lee into the community of scholars as a mature, albeit very junior, scholar in his own right.

Conclusion

We understand that students follow a variety of steps in writing their research papers and that success relies primarily on two things:

- The student's "maturity"—including academic mechanics but also a more mature interest in the topic and a readiness to devote the time and attention that good work requires
- The student's "connection"—the degree to which the student sees and enters into the network of scholars working on the same or related projects, whether through face-to-face relationships or through reading

We also understand that instructors set the criteria in varying ways but generally want a well-written paper that demonstrates an understanding and integration of the work of experts in

the field into a cogent argument. "Success" may mean as little as completing the assignment and getting an acceptable grade or as much as writing a publishable or presentable paper.

Librarians want to meet the needs of all students, whether they aspire merely to complete an assignment or to make their mark and enter a scholarly field themselves. What, then, can the library do to help the range of students? How can the library help students find themselves whether they are research-oriented scholars like Abbie and Lee or practical and job-oriented like Danielle, Tiffany, and Tanya?

The key to writing a good undergraduate research paper, it seems, is to be engaged with and interested in the topic. In general, students who were more interested in their papers found better resources, obtained more assistance in finding resources and writing, started working on the assignments earlier, were more likely to make use of the library, and wrote better papers. The more engaged students assumed that the information they needed existed and it was up to them to find it (with assistance if necessary), while the less engaged students tended to assume that if they could not find information on a topic, it did not exist.

It seems then that one way to help students write better papers would be to help them find better topics within the constraints of the courses they are taking. In this the library may be able to assist, but it would require greater cooperation between subject librarians, library staff, and instructors. As librarians and library staff thought about this possibility, they imagined several ways in which the findings could lead to improvements.

Librarians can act on the understanding that academic maturity and success depend on overall maturity by seeking ways to work with such student services as academic advising and residential life to integrate the library into other college-provided support services.

Librarians can build on the understanding that many students have an extremely scant foundation of knowledge in the field of their assigned research paper and have difficulty finding and assessing resources. For example, they can help students address this problem by encouraging them to use the "peer review/scholarly" filter in databases. Librarians can develop ways to help students identify the aspects of their projects that are most intellectually exciting to them so that in even a small way they can activate an intrinsic motivation to explore the topic.

With regard to connecting students to experts in their fields, librarians can help students develop their ability to connect with their instructors by sponsoring casual get-togethers or by acting as mentors in 100-level courses. They can ease students into scholarly networks by displaying the work of visiting researchers and speakers and encouraging students to attend events where they can meet these people and learn about their work. They can expose students to models of successful "academic maturity" by sponsoring talks in which interesting, eminent faculty members discuss what they do and how they found themselves and matured intellectually and in life.

Just understanding the student work process and gaining the insights provided by our close studies of work practices can help librarians and library staff on the many occasions, large and small, in which they find themselves working with students and augers well for future improvements in the library.

Appendix 8A. Retrospective Interview Protocol

Introduce yourselves and tell the student you are interested in what students really do when they write their papers. Review the information sheet and make sure the student understands that participation is voluntary and that we may use excerpts of the transcript or an image of the drawing in presentations or publications, to illustrate our methods or findings. Have the student complete the receipt and give the student $20.

Question: What research papers did you write last semester? (Write on back of drawing paper)

Explain: We'll be talking about one paper: the one you wrote for [course]. I'd like you to draw a picture of the writing of this paper while we talk.

Question: How did you receive the assignment? Draw or note yourself receiving the assignment.

Question: What was the very first thing you did? When was it?

Question: What was the next thing you did? [Note: have student indicate the passage of time with an arrow. Indicate how much time has passed between steps, or when the step occurred, to the extent that the student can remember.]

[Continue with this question until the student indicates that the paper is handed in]

Question: May I ask, how did you do on this paper? What helped you do as well as you did? What would have helped you do better?

Question: The next time you do a paper, will you try to do anything different?

Notes

1. For more information on this project, see "The Social Life of Grey Literature: Work Practice Study to Improve Institutional Repositories" (LG-02-03-0129-03).

2. For a discussion of student photographs, see Chapter 4, "Picture My Work." We discuss student development in Chapter 5, "Learning the Ropes" and how people seek information in Chapters 6 and 7, "'Whatever Works': Finding Trusted Information" and "Research as Connection."

3. We learned of this method from OCLC's Merrilee Proffitt, who was then working on the RedLightGreen project (http://www.oclc.org/research/activities/redlightgreen.html).

4. "Abbie" and other student names are pseudonyms. All other information in the student profiles is accurate; details are removed to preserve anonymity.

5. For more information about faculty expectation interviews, see Chapter 2, "Hallmarks of a Good Paper."

References

Alvarez, B. & Dimmock,N. (2007). Faculty expectations of student research. In N.F. Foster & S. Gibbons (Eds.), *Studying students: The undergraduate research project at the University of Rochester* (pp. 1–6). Chicago, IL: Association of College and Research Libraries.

Bell, S. & Unsworth, A. (2007). Night owl librarians: Shifting the reference clock. In N.F. Foster & S. Gibbons (Eds.), *Studying students: The undergraduate research project at the University of Rochester* (pp. 16–19). Chicago, IL: Association of College and Research Libraries.

Foster, N.F. & Gibbons, S. (2005). Understanding faculty to improve content recruitment for institutional repositories. *D-Lib Magazine, 11*(1). Retrieved from http://www.dlib.org/dlib/january05/foster/01foster.html

Foster, N.F. & Gibbons, S. (Eds.) (2007). *Studying students: The undergraduate research project at the University of Rochester*. Retrieved from UR Research website: http://hdl.handle.net/1802/7520

Gibbons, S. & Foster, N.F. (2007). Conclusion: Creating student-centered academic libraries. In N.F. Foster & S. Gibbons (Eds.), *Studying students: The undergraduate research project at the University of Rochester* (pp. 79–83). Chicago, IL: Association of College and Research Libraries.

chapter nine. Designing Academic Libraries with the People Who Work in Them

Nancy Fried Foster

In unstable times a physical re-programming can no longer depend on traditional, professional experts (architects and librarians), for whom precedent is now unreliable. We looked to our user community's expertise.

~ David Cronrath, Dean
School of Architecture
Planning & Preservation
University of Maryland

The old way is over; we do not use academic libraries as we once did, and we no longer turn their design over to a few "experts." But what is the new way? In this chapter, I describe an alternative, called participatory design, that engages a wide range of experts in the design process and yields an academic library suited to the needs of all the people—faculty members, students, and library staff—who will work in it.

In the following pages, I start with a selective look at approaches to library design described in the literature of the past 80 years, tracing the emergence of an interest in participatory processes with an emphasis on accommodating people's work practices. I discuss projects we have completed at the University of Rochester to illustrate this process and conclude with questions about the future of academic library buildings and how we might investigate alternative futures in a participatory fashion.

Traditions of Academic Library Design

In 1932, James Gerould criticized the planning of academic libraries in earlier times when he wrote, "Frequently the architect and donor were more interested in erecting a monument than a working [academic library] building" (p. 8). The process he described took little account of local needs:

> A few notes, together with the limit of cost, are turned over to the architect; and he is expected to produce a proper building. Generally he is even less advised as to the business of the library than is his client. He turns over the pages of his journals, studies the design of such buildings as he may come across, perhaps visits a few that are in the vicinity—most of which are probably the result of the same type of planning—draws his own sketches, and they are accepted. (Gerould, 1932, pp. 15–16).

Better, he argued, to follow the example of Dartmouth College, where a faculty committee had conducted a study at the request of the trustees and provided a 22-page report on what would be required of the new library (Gerould, 1932, pp. 16–17). But this was a rare approach. According to the literature from the early to mid-twentieth century, a very limited number of people participated in the design of academic libraries, although Gerould and other enlightened contemporaries saw great value in developing library plans in response to local conditions and needs. Of course, these conditions and needs were usually imagined within narrow limits: topography and architectural style of the campus; size and constitution of student body;

and subjects taught. The main concerns appear to have been that the library fit in with the rest of the campus and that it be large enough to accommodate a geometrically expanding number of volumes.

Only some in the field saw the value of including the librarian in the design process (Larson & Palmer, 1933, p. 77ff). Hanley and others delineated the uses of the college or university library building: acquiring and maintaining the collection; providing materials when required; providing spaces for reading and studying; making individual studies available to researchers; providing "assistance in developing the reading habit;" and "acquainting of the users with the contents of the library." Hanley argued that,

> The arrangement for the handling of these functions and their supplementary factors depends on the cooperative program outlined by the librarian, the faculty, and the president, and on the ingenuity of the architect, the specific variations and adaptations for particular requirements, and the amount of money at the disposal of the builder. (1939, p. 11)

The precise methods for including the librarian and the faculty in the development of the program are not laid out in any of these guides and one is left to imagine a combination of committee work and the solicitation of suggestions and comments. That is, there is every indication that the most senior leaders of the university along with the university librarian or library dean were the client group with whom the architects worked, perhaps with the help of a building consultant. It was the top people who made the decisions.

By 1960, the library held not just books and journals on paper but microforms, and the age of computers was dawning. An interesting book written more than 50 years ago by Ralph Ellsworth, remembered as the head of the University of Colorado Library, is startling in its attention to issues we think of as purely contemporary. Ellsworth wanted libraries to be large enough to accommodate both the geometrically growing collections of academic libraries and the explosion in enrollments. He wanted to include a wide range of non-book media in academic library collections, and he wanted to build libraries to accommodate changes in pedagogy.

Evidence of Ellsworth's modernity was his vision of libraries as work and research spaces rather than as the only place the collections could be consulted. He wrote,

> When the microcard was introduced we envisioned the time when we would give each entering freshman, to keep in his dormitory room, a complete college library in the form of a few shoe boxes of microcards and we expected to turn our central library buildings into purely research centers, but we have failed to do this, not because the idea was unsound but because we failed to develop good reading machines, and because of the economics of the problem. (Ellsworth, 1960, p. 10)

Ellsworth had a surprising sensitivity to the needs of students and faculty members, writing, for example, that "librarians who fail to make it possible for scientists to get at their literature late at night and on weekends are asking for trouble" (Ellsworth 1960, p. 19). And again,

> Most college libraries try to provide group discussion and conference rooms near the reading areas where the young students find their assigned reading books…. If possible smoking should be permitted in them and they should have good sound deadening qualities because the talking will be noisy. The door should have a large window in it. (Ellsworth, 1960, pp. 72–73)

Ellsworth argued strongly for the constitution of a faculty library planning committee as well as a student committee to advise the librarian. He also recommended the use of a consultant for "new ideas, trends and the best thinking and experience that can be provided. He can suggest buildings for them to visit.... The local committee, in turn, can educate the consultant on matters of local traditions, backgrounds and the unique characteristics of the institution" (Ellsworth, 1960, p. 27). Similarly, Metcalf's classic *Planning Academic and Research Library Buildings* suggests that trustees, administrators, faculty, students, and even librarians be included on planning teams (Metcalf, 1965, p. 240).

Cohen and Cohen worked in the same vein as their predecessors, adding a distinctive and welcome sensitivity to human needs in shared space (Cohen & Cohen, 1979). In their guidance on writing the program, Cohen and Cohen stress size and growth of the collection but they also include a step to identify what people will actually do in the library. Specifically, they recommend answering the following questions: "How is work done in the library? What tasks are involved in the staff areas and how must they fit together? Will equipment replace some functions? How will this affect the space allocation or power requirements?" (Cohen & Cohen, 1979, p. 38). These excellent questions reflect the state of the art: a focus on the functional requirements of keeping a library open. They recommend visualizing the completed space by making a "mental" walk through, "first as a user and then as a staff member" (Cohen and Cohen 1979, p. 72).

The next great innovation, the "charrette," appears in the library literature by the 1990s. In a 1991 article, Healy explained,

"Charrette" is a French word meaning "cart." It came into use in architectural parlance in the early 1900s at the Ecole des Beaux-

Arts in Paris. Studio projects were assigned to students, with a deadline for completing the project and turning it in, usually in 12 to 24 hours. Often these projects were due at midnight. Students traditionally worked feverishly, right up to the last minute, when a cart was wheeled down the aisles between the drafting tables. Their drawings were hastily placed in the cart—sometimes with a student or two riding the cart down the aisles putting the final touches on a drawing. (p. 302)

Healy goes on to explain that the charrette came to designate a special kind of work session, held toward the end of a design process, in which members of a community would be invited to give feedback on the plans that the architects had developed up to that point and make additional suggestions. "Each group," he says, "was asked for its particular concerns and was invited to come back at any time during the charrette to see how we had dealt with their input" (Healy, 1991, p. 304). He argues that this approach has great advantages, quoting the director of a library that was designed this way:

Everyone got caught up in the excitement and enthusiasm of the charrette. When they realized that their ideas were being considered and they were being listened to, they were anxious to come back the next morning to see what new developments had taken place overnight. (Healey 1991, p. 304)

Note that the community is asked for "its particular concerns"—the emphasis is on collecting information about what people care about, are concerned about, or need (Healey, 1991, p. 304). I will contrast this, below, with the participatory design approach, which asks members of the community to participate as experts who provide information about their work practices.

The charrette is discussed a year later by Carmack, who mentions "users" in a review of the people who should be involved in a library planning project (Carmack, 1992). He encourages the inclusion of faculty members and students as well as librarians, writing,

> Politically, in this day of shared governance, to use an academic term, building a library building without involving the library staff in a meaningful way is sheer folly. In all but the smallest libraries there is going to exist a cadre of talent, expertise, and experience that will be useful to the project. This expertise and experience can be useful in the fact-finding process, in the development of the program statement, in the selling of the project and in public relations. (Carmack, 1992, p. 27)

Overall, there is an emphasis on the value of including people outside of the library leadership team in the design process both because they have valuable advice to give and because they will, in turn, help to "sell" the project to other community members.

In our 2005 Gleason Library project, we described our own approach as a charrette (Gibbons & Foster, 2007). We recognized the value of ignoring our own assumptions and finding ways to see and understand student work practices, although we were still primarily interested in what our students might need, rather than what they needed to do. Our main information gathering activities were design workshops, observations, and the gathering of student input on flip charts.

The charrette concept has endured in the library literature, showing up more recently in the work of Somerville and Brown-Sica. They describe the charrette and its value as follows:

> Today, the term refers to professionals and interested parties engaging in a condensed, interactive design process. Properly conducted, a charette [sic] encourages

open communication to explore ideas and exchange viewpoints, which are illustrated in architectural terms as lines and shapes on paper. By contrast, the conventional approach to library planning occurs in an architect's office, in the absence of the clients (library staff and library beneficiaries). (Somerville & Brown-Sica, 2011, p. 673)

Citing Beard and Dale (2010), Somerville and Brown-Sica (2011) note the singular importance of basing all such work on a knowledge of "what the student does" (p. 676).

Underlying the more recent approaches is an emerging attention to work practices echoing Webb who argues that library buildings should be designed to accommodate mission-related activities. Webb explains,

> The "function" that any architectural form is supposed to follow is determined, of course, by the activities to be performed in the finished building. The activities, in turn, derive from the mission of the organization that occupies the building. While it is true that some avant-garde architects have emphasized form at the expense of functionality, it is still the point that a house is a residence, a church is for worship, and an office building is for conducting business. In a sense, architecture is like a folk art in which the art objects, though decorated and beautified, are nonetheless initiated for utilitarian purposes. (2004, pp. 7–8)

As the years go by and the mission of the library is taken less and less for granted, these words remain compelling but become harder to put into practice.

Participatory Design in Practice at the River Campus Libraries

Our approach to the design of library spaces at the University of Rochester's River Campus

Libraries has been influenced by the more recent literature on library design, such as the influential CLIR report on the "Library as Place" (Bennett, 2005) and the reports of librarians at the University of Queensland (e.g., Webster, 2010) among many others. We have also benefitted from interchange with concurrent projects at other universities, such as the reprogramming of McKeldin Library at the University of Maryland (Steele & Foster, 2012) and the design of the Active Learning Center at Purdue University (Foster et al., 2013).[1]

Our approach has changed over the past nine years as we have used ethnographic methods to understand how faculty members, students, and our own staff members do their library-related work. In a nutshell, we have moved from the charrette-type approach described above, which we used in our Gleason Library renovation, to a more explicit participatory design approach that focuses, as Webb says, on supporting the mission-related activities in which people engage in the building.

We wrote about the process and outcomes of the Gleason Library design project in *Studying Students*; since publication of that book, we have assessed and updated the space using participatory methods. While there was no formal post-occupancy evaluation, we conducted two informal assessments.

For the first assessment, we placed two flip-charts in the space. On one, we asked, "What do you like best about the Gleason Library?" and on the other we asked, "What else do you want in the Gleason Library?" In response to the latter question, we learned that students wanted more food and coffee; better separation between the noisier and the quieter sub-areas within the space; many more whiteboards; and more computers. We were able to meet some of these needs immediately and have continued to address others as time, resources, and priorities allow.

Figure 9.1. Group study area in the Gleason Library

Figure 9.2. Original lounge area in the Gleason Library

We pulled out a list of the top themes of the drawings students had made in the design workshops we conducted as part of the initial participatory design process. We then compared that list to the flipchart responses regarding the best things about the renovated space. This comparison suggests that people using the space experienced a match between their needs and the Gleason Library's affordances (see Table 9.1). At the time, we used the language of *things* in our analyses and interpretations. That is, we looked for the things people needed (light, furnishings, meeting rooms) rather than the activities they needed to conduct (seeing what they were reading, seeing each other, seeing to the outside world). However, even though our method was not yet very evolved, we were able to capture and act on subtle information. For example, one of our top themes was "sybaritic area." This category comprised numerous drawing elements that represented a need to be calm, free of stress, and secure as well as focused and intellectually stimulated. (Drawing elements in this category included massage rooms, a padded room for punching, fountains and fish ponds, expensive carpeting and woodwork, leather-bound books, inspiring quotations, and so on.) In other words, we were able to accomplish one of the prime goals of participatory design albeit in an unsophisticated way; we were able to provide a space to support work practices that we discovered through engagement with the appropriate experts: the students.

We also conducted a series of observations that included tallies of people in the space and their activities as well as impressionistic descriptions of noise and activity levels, temperature, odors, and other sensory information. We were gratified to see that students made heavy use of almost every single area of the new space, primarily for such academic work as reading, writing, doing group projects, and working out math, physics, and music problems on whiteboards.

Table 9.1. Comparison of themes in students' design workshop drawings to comments on post-occupancy flipcharts

Top Themes from Design Workshop Drawings	Top Comments on Post-Occupancy Flipcharts
• Windows/light	• Windows/light
• Comfy area(s) with sofas, chairs, tables	• Seating (comfort/variety/arrangement)
• Group-study areas, meeting rooms	• Group study areas (enclosed spaces)
• Quiet-study area	• Quiet area
• Sybaritic area	• I can do work now/relaxing/not too quiet and not too noisy/happy
• Computer area	• Whiteboards/write-able walls
• Café, snack shop, vending	• Open 24 hours
• Individual study area	• Spacious/room between people/high ceilings
	• Colors/décor

But we were surprised to discover that one particular area of the Gleason Library, a lounge area with couches and two large screens, was markedly underutilized. We resolved to re-design that sub-space to respond better to student needs.

To do this, we conducted a very quick, onsite design workshop with randomly selected students who were in the Gleason Library. An analysis of these drawings suggested that students needed even more places to work in groups. Secondarily, they needed access to screens into which they could plug a laptop. By coincidence, another campus unit had tables to spare and sought couches for a lounge-like area. We were able to make a no-cost trade and reconfigure this corner of the Gleason Library. It is well used now according to subsequent observations.

Figure 9.3. Additional group study area in what was originally a lounge area in the Gleason Library

A Place for Graduate Students to Get Away

To visit the Gleason Library early in the day is to see a just a few people, a bit older looking, spread out and working quietly and alone. But as the day wears on, the population of the space looks younger, gets noisier and more active, and increases in number until by late evening the space feels at or beyond capacity. These are ideal conditions for many undergraduates but intolerable ones for most graduate students.

We had conducted a participatory design project with graduate students from 2006 to 2008 to improve our institutional repository (Randall, Clark, Smith, & Foster, 2008). Although we were designing a software tool at the time, we gained insight on graduate student work practices and the activities and states of mind they needed their workspaces to afford. One key finding was that graduate students served as instructors and TAs and spent a great deal of time preparing, teaching, and responding to the needs of undergraduates in those college courses. Graduate students, we learned, desperately needed an escape from undergraduates, that is, a place to do their own course work and write their own papers without interruption. Through the generosity of a University of Rochester Life Trustee, Martin E. Messinger, we were able to provide not one but two such spaces.

To design the new Messinger Graduate Studies, we conducted a quick design workshop with graduate students in one of the two designated spaces. We asked students to draw an ideal layout for the space and we debriefed students on the drawings, adding notes to their papers for future analysis. We also asked students to comment on several possible designs that a professional interior designer had prepared for us. Student responses to the professional designs provided additional insights into the types of activities they expected to do in the space and the qualities that would allow them to be successful in those activities.

Figure 9.4. North Messinger Graduate Study

Figure 9.5. South Messinger Graduate Study

Based on these insights, we developed new designs for the two rooms, planning one as a very quiet area and the other as a somewhat less quiet area that would be appropriate for group work. We believed that group work space was a significant need because we had detected a growth in dissertation writing groups and other collaborative groups in our original project (Randall et al., 2008, p. 2). Once we had completed a basic design, we further engaged students in selecting furnishings, carpeting, and the color schemes for the two rooms.

After occupancy, we wondered whether and how the rooms were being used. We knew that there was a waiting list for the lockers that we provided in both studies, but we were not convinced that many students used the rooms. A quick set of observations in the spring semester of 2013 confirmed that the rooms were well used but only for individual work. Contrary to our initial assumption, we now believe that neither room is large enough to support group work. In the far larger Gleason Library, activity and noise provide cover for numerous groups. By contrast, the Messinger Studies are intimate spaces in which a small group attracts attention and creates a distraction for anyone else in the room. We revised our expectations for these rooms but decided to collect additional information from the graduate students working in them to see what they liked and what more they needed. We discovered that students were by and large happy with the rooms, and especially happy that they provided a quiet place away from undergraduates. They were dissatisfied with heating and cooling and with cleanliness of the rooms, issues that we addressed at once.

Differences between the initial design process, on the one hand, and later assessment of the spaces, on the other, illustrate the difference between participatory and other user-centered approaches to design. We call it participatory design when we engage the people who will use the space in generative, communicative activities that enable them to share their expertise about their own work practices. In drawing a picture of an ideal space and discussing it with a facilitator, the work-practice expert (such as a graduate student) uses a mediating object—the picture—and a human mediator, the facilitator—to translate and share that expertise in a way that other experts (such as architects or interior designers) can understand. Asking people to voice their preferences regarding furnishings, carpeting, and so on is different. While stylistic preferences could in some instances be used as fodder for analysis and interpretation, in this instance they were used in a straightforward manner to complete the planning of the rooms. The resulting spaces were configured to support identified work practices and were furnished and finished to suit the tastes of the majority.

Participatory Design of Science Libraries

Several libraries within our overall River Campus Libraries system cater to people who use online resources predominantly or exclusively. Two of these are the Carlson Science and Engineering Library and the Physics-Optics-Astronomy Library (POA). Other campus departments, realizing that patterns of library use have changed with the advent of digital resources, have advanced claims on these library spaces, proposing to covert them into faculty offices or laboratories for computation or bench science. These proposals prompted us to ask whether it still makes sense to keep science libraries open.

Keeping the libraries open certainly runs counter to the recent trend of consolidation and closure of science libraries at major American universities. Sometimes the budget forces an academic library system to consolidate and close branches (Steussy, 2009); sometimes academic departments move and a departmental library makes less sense (Twiss-Brooks, 2005);

sometimes it seems that no one is using paper anymore so libraries go all-digital (Petroski, 2008; Martinez, 2010).

Librarians at Cornell tracked branch closures at academic libraries and found that closures in physical sciences, life sciences and engineering vastly outnumbered those in social sciences and arts (see Table 9.2).

Table 9.2. Branch closures in academic libraries (reproduced from Cornell University Library Research and Assessment Unit, 2009)

Major Subject Area	% of Branch Closures
Physical Sciences (Physics, Chemistry, Astronomy, Geology)	40
Social Sciences	18
Life Sciences (Biology, Agriculture, Forestry, Fisheries)	14
Math	11
Arts (Art, Music, Design)	8
Engineering	6
Health Sciences (Medicine, Dentistry)	3

A Physical Library for People Who Use Online Resources

We felt the pressure at the University of Rochester and wondered whether we were right to keep our Carlson Science and Engineering Library open. We knew that people were in the building so we knew that it was used, but we wondered whether it was *well* used. To find out, a small team of librarians and library staff took a closer look from the spring of 2009 until the spring of 2010, using the ethnographic methods we had already developed in our research on faculty members and students. Our objective was to understand the use that is made of Carlson Library, especially by the students who are its most frequent patrons. Surprisingly, we found that this particular space is defined by its physical collections, even when patrons make only sporadic use of them.

Methods[2]

For this project, a team of seven librarians and staff members utilized four methods developed in the course of our ongoing work.[3]

The first method, reply cards, entailed the distribution by library staff of mini-questionnaires, printed on cards, to people in the library on two days late in the Spring 2009 semester and on one day in the Fall 2010 semester and the analysis of the completed cards that were returned to the desk. In addition to requesting student or faculty status, department or major, and expected year of graduation, we asked five questions:

- What are you doing here in this seat right now?
- How long have you been here?
- Why are you here and not someplace else?
- If we made you move this minute, where would you go?
- When is the very last time you were in this seat (or one right by it)?

The first time we distributed cards in only one area of the library, but the second time we chose six separate locations throughout all three floors of the library. We coded and quantified the answers to the questions on the reply cards to discern who was using the library—undergraduates, graduate students, faculty members, or other individuals—to learn what people were doing in the library and to understand why they had chosen that particular library space for that activity.

The second method, a design workshop in June 2009, engaged 20 library users in an activity to draw a "perfect" configuration for the first floor of Carlson Library. We analyzed the drawings in a group brainstorming session, focusing on recurring elements to identify the academic and other activities that students need to do in the space. The drawings that students completed in the design workshop were broken down into elements that we clustered into categories related to work tasks and requirements.

Onsite interviews of nine students during the 2009–2010 academic year constituted the third method. We interviewed three students about one particular visit to the library ("log interviews") and six of them about previous use of the library ("walkthrough interviews"). Interviews were coded and counted to assess which parts of the library had been used by the interviewed individuals and for what purposes. These interviews also allowed us to probe student attitudes towards different features of the library, including physical collections and different sub-spaces.

Finally, using our fourth method we conducted observations three times a day, at 2:00 p.m., 6:00 p.m., and 10:00 p.m., over a full week early in the Spring 2009 semester from February 11–17. All team members participated in this activity, using an observation sheet and detailed floor plans. Analysis of observation data was done in an Excel spreadsheet in which we embedded formulas to track the ebb and flow of traffic over the course of the week and from one area to another as well as to calculate the number of individuals engaged in academic or recreational tasks at the moment of observation.

In the Library but Not Using the Books

We felt that the information drawn from reply cards, drawings, interviews and observations, augmented with spontaneous questioning for clarification, gave us a good sense of the people who were in the Carlson Library and what they were doing there. We saw and spoke mainly with undergraduates in the sciences, working individually, who needed to study for exams; complete homework assignments; read books, journals, PDFs, and other materials, both in print and on the screen; work on research papers and research-based assignments; do challenging intellectual work, such as a calculations or equations; and occasionally use reserve materials, especially textbooks. In addition, but in fewer numbers, students worked in small groups and needed to have discussions; receive or provide instruction; and work on group projects and assignments.

Library collections, staff, space, equipment, and furnishings support people in these activities. Our analyses enabled us to identify a wide range of important supports, starting with the proximity of resources and reference materials, whether over the Internet using a public workstation or one's own laptop or using a printed reference work, journal, or textbook. The availability of help from a professional librarian or a library staff member or student, whether to get specialized information, find an item in the collection, or borrow a laptop lock, was also important. We saw that students need to work in well-lit, quiet, comfortable places; to use a range of seating types; and to lie down or calm down occasionally, for example by working on a jigsaw puzzle. They need to use computers, print, scan, and power their own equipment.

The people who use Carlson Library need whiteboards or some other technology that allows them to work out their ideas and solve problems on a large, writable surface. Large tables support group work or the spreading out of a large number of materials, and these are heavily used. Carrels and desks give individuals a place to work alone, without interruption; they draw students in large numbers. We found that the contiguous arrangement of various furnishings made it possible for students to move among spaces that support different tasks or to work in a space that was suitable for their own work while remaining close to friends doing different work. The arrangement of physical collections throughout the space puts students and others in the library close to important books, articles, and reference works. Few use these books, but many feel they create a physical environment that incorporates scientists through the presence of their work and helps students enter this scientific community

Figure 9.6. Prized window seating in Carlson Science and Engineering Library

Figure 9.7. Carrels buffered by stacks in Carlson Science and Engineering Library

Importantly, we noted that many and possibly all students who use Carlson Library alternate between academic activities and recreational ones. We observed that some students were studying while others were on YouTube or Facebook and also that individuals were moving back and forth between academic and recreational tasks, such as socializing or working on a jigsaw puzzle. Comparing the counts of students engaged in these different activities yields an almost 6:1 ratio of academic to recreational activities, confirming for us that students are using the space mainly to do their academic work.

Our research revealed that some people who came to the library were doing academic activities that could only be done in the library: using library resources and services. It would seem that others could use any space with the convenience and affordances of the library, even if the space did not provide collections or services. However, we saw evidence in our research to support the view that even those students who were not obviously using library collections or services were benefitting from being in the library, as opposed to being in a study space in some other building. Much of this evidence came from the drawings of "perfect library spaces" and the conversations we had with students who drew the pictures, as well as from the "walkthrough" and "log" interviews. In particular we found that students wanted to study amid the collections. While some wanted only to benefit from the sound-damping physicality of these materials, most wanted to be close to journals, textbooks, and reference books, even if they used them only occasionally or only online. The students' manifest explanation was that they wanted to be in a place with the sort of scholarly gravitas that the library affords; they said it made them more serious.

Updating the Physics-Optics-Astronomy Library

Shortly after we completed our study of the Carlson Science Library, we found out that another science library, Physics-Optics-Astronomy (POA), would be closed at the end of the spring semester.[4] POA is a branch library located in Bausch & Lomb Hall, the home of the Phys-

Figure 9.8. The Physics-Optics-Astronomy Library

ics and Astronomy Department. Originally a departmental library that was used mainly by faculty members and graduate students, it had been all but ceded to undergraduates as researchers turned increasingly to online literature.

POA was one of the first places prospective students were shown on a tour of the physics department, to give them a sense of life as a physics student at the University. Physics and astronomy majors used the place heavily; it was a home away from home. To close it struck many as a devastating loss.

The argument to close it was strong. The University urgently needed space for new faculty offices, laboratories, and classrooms. In particular, the engineering school needed space for a new computer classroom. Space planners and university administrators believed that there was little use for a physical library for physics, even less than for other science fields because physics has long been a leader in online access to the literature. Whatever could not be made available online could be moved to the Carlson Science and Engineering Library, they reasoned. Library administration advocated for keeping POA open,

but university administration was adamant until word got out about the proposed closing and physics students, faculty, and alumni sprang into action. They wrote letters, made posters, and created a Facebook page to protest the decision. As the president of the Society for Physics Students wrote, "We must be able to explain *not* why the POA is a good library but why its existence is incredibly beneficial to physics students of all types." On Facebook, a student commented, "Remember: They aren't just removing a library, they are displacing a *community*." And an alumnus summed it up, saying, "The close proximity of the reserve book collection to the group study area, the centrality of its location, its facilitation of student/grad-student/professor interactions, and to remain competitive with other institutions are just a few of the reasons. But the real reason the room should not be closed is the intense focused scholarship that occurs there … It is that room which, like a lens, focuses intense academic activity into heightened student performance and lasting activity."[5]

In the end, a different space was found for the computer lab and POA remains open. Saved from a close call and excited to learn just how much POA meant to so many people, library administration decided to update the space using a participatory design approach. We held an hour-long design workshop with 24 undergraduates and one grad student, recruiting participants through a poster and the offer of free pizza and drinks. Following past practice, we gave each student a piece of poster paper, some Post-Its, and colored markers; asked them to imagine that they could redesign the space any way they wanted; and had them draw whatever they imagined. In addition to their pictures, we collected some information from workshop participants about their recent use of libraries, the library website, and scholarly literature.

Almost every student, 23 of 25, had been in POA within past 24 hours, and before that, within the previous two days, for an average stay of about four hours. Almost every student, 24 of 25, had also been in another library on campus within the past week or so. However, although they were frequent users of POA and other libraries, they did not borrow books very often. It had been about a month, on average, since anyone had borrowed a textbook and about three months since anyone had borrowed another kind of book. Although they were not heavy users of physical books, many of them read the literature online. Nine had accessed online literature the day of the workshop and another eight had read online literature within the prior week. We also learned that a large majority of respondents had consulted online literature late at night, between midnight and 6:00 a.m.

When we analyzed the students' drawings, we learned that they wanted to be able to study and read; use computers, printers, and copiers; and work alone and in groups, using reference or reserve materials from time to time. Beyond that, we found that they wanted to be able to relax and socialize in the space and feel a sense of pride and connection to the department and to each other as a group of physics and astronomy students. We also learned that teaching and learning from each other was an important activity for them and they wanted the space to support that. Additionally, they wanted to be able to work for a long time in the space, preferably with access to snacks and coffee.

By moving some of the less-used journals to offsite shelving, we were able to create a nicer space near the library entrance for relaxing and socializing and some new nooks for group tables and quiet work. Students have responded by using the library in consistently high numbers. Faculty members have responded by piloting the teaching of a "flipped" course in POA with great success.

Science Libraries: Broader Questions

It may be that studying in the library is itself part of becoming a scientist. The library may provide the setting, props, and people that students need to adopt the habitus, that is, to acquire the habits of mind and ways of being in the world that can only be learned through participation in a scholarly community. Maintenance of the group is a very important part of this, and we see students using the affordances of the space to keep their study and other groups intact, even while group members are engaged in different

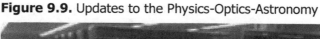

Figure 9.9. Updates to the Physics-Optics-Astronomy

activities. Working in the scholarly setting among other undergraduates, graduate students, and the occasional faculty member helps less experienced students develop good work patterns and rhythms and learn how and when to consult library staff and use library resources.

Carlson Library affords students with both a place to consult library materials and personnel and an environment in which to focus on their work and learn how to be academics. This is in addition to a service the library offers to the university community by simply providing study space that is not currently available elsewhere. POA likewise provides study space and more: It is where even a beginning student in an introductory physics class can feel like part of the discipline. If more study spaces were to be built elsewhere on campus, we might see reduced use of these two libraries, but there are unique aspects to the Carlson and POA Libraries that we believe would still draw large numbers of students. These aspects center on the seriousness that is supported by the library as a whole and include the presence of the physical collections, and the fact that students can alternate between isolated quiet work and group discussion—all within a space physically marked out by shelves of books and periodicals and appointed with other indicators of the work of illustrious scientists. In this unique space, students can consult library materials and experience a connection to past and current scientists and the larger community of science majors, teaching assistants, graduate students, and faculty members in the sciences. Students can also see the physical products of scientific studies, much as humanities and social science students see the classic works and artistic creations of people in their field, thus developing further a sense of belonging to a tradition and a vital, productive endeavor.

The Future of Library Buildings

As more and more of the scholarly literature in scientific fields is available online, it makes sense to ask what science libraries are for and whether they should still be built or maintained. To explore these issues is to raise questions about academic libraries in general and about the processes by which we might successfully design them, if indeed we do continue to design them.

In the last regard, our experience with POA is instructive. In a sense, the existence of POA at all seems at least in part due to the energetic and vociferous *participation* of a range of interested parties in a campaign to keep it open. POA was found to be an inappropriate site for the proposed computer lab and, at least officially, this is what saved the library. However, there was widespread belief that the protests of faculty members, students, and alumni played a significant role in the university administration's change of course. They did not actually design the library, but they built and documented a case for its existence, a case that included many clear statements of what people felt the library, more than any other place, enabled them to do. This in itself covered much of the ground of a participatory design process. What it lacked was what happened in the follow-on, library-led participatory design of the POA renovation. In that project, librarians developed requirements with students who would use the space and shared them with the people who developed specifications and building plans. Put together, this project comprised the most important aspects of participatory design. It was driven by the people who had the greatest stake. Numbers of different stakeholders provided information about their work practices and needs. Other individuals provided expertise in such important areas as construction and interior design. A central facilitator enabled information exchange among these parties in a way that privileged the practices and needs of those who would work in the renovated space.

A participatory process could be used to ask whether any academic library should remain open or be built or renovated and then to develop the requirements and specifications for construction and finishing. This chapter has provided many examples of renovation projects; I would like to conclude by speculating about using participatory design to make decisions about the future of the library.

I can imagine creating a set of participatory activities through which a number of stakeholder groups could envision and then share information about their current and prospective needs with regard to scholarly communication and literature; their own research, teaching, and learning practices; technology for research, teaching, and learning; access; preservation; and a number of other topics that relate directly to the work of the wide range of faculty members, students, library staff, and others who do some or all of their work in the library building or with resources that the library provides.

In the analysis, I can imagine investigating the ways in which work practices and needs line up with what we currently think of as libraries as well as with a large number of other places, institutions, resources, technologies, and services. We might come away with a very different perspective on academic libraries.

We might decide to devote the library *qua* building exclusively to three things: research on physical collections; face-to-face consultation about the collections and special technologies to find and use them; and teaching with the collections. That is, the library might become a place of books all over again.

We might decide to help the University upgrade other, non-library campus spaces, including classroom buildings, for use as study halls, that is, as high-quality spaces that afford group and individual work; quiet and noisy work; short stays and long, concentrated periods of study; simple reading and writing as well as work that requires power, Internet connectivity, hardware, software; and other supports that speak to the findings of this volume.

We might decide to re-create departmental libraries by taking advantage of the latest technologies, which allow us to bring resources and special services into any space, anytime. A few laptops or tablets, a table or two, and the scheduled presence of the library's subject specialists and suddenly anthropology, biology, history, mechanical engineering, and statistics would all have their own libraries right in their own departments.

We might decide to redeploy library staff away from managing general study areas and toward the development of new technologies that use library metadata in new ways. For example, we might conclude that libraries should lead the development of new, transformed metadata standards and new applications and apps that would let us aggregate and expose resources from library and non-library collections for our students, faculty members, researchers, and the world.

And we might not. But we would have an enormous, relevant set of data from participating members of our academic community to mine for information about our own future.

As David Cronrath says, "precedent is unreliable." Fortunately, we have a way to build the future of libraries together with all the people who use them. Using the methods of participatory design, we can design academic libraries with the people who work in them.

Notes

1. These and many more resources that have influenced our work can be found in the Zotero bibliography for the "AnthroLib" group (http://www.zotero.org/groups/28707).

2. We are indebted to Keith Webster and librarians at the University of Queensland for many of the methods used in this study.

3. Team members included Helen Anderson, Marylou Biedenbach, Diane Cass, Katie Clark, Nancy Foster, Kenn Harper, and Trina Lowry.

4. This section draws heavily from notes prepared by Pat Sulouff, retired head of the POA Library.

5. Comments appeared on a "Fight for the POA" Facebook page.

References

Beard, J., & Dale, D. (2010). Library design, learning spaces and academic literacy. *New Library World 111,* (11/12), 480–492. doi:http://dx.doi.org.ezp.lib.rochester.edu/10.1108/03074801011094859

Bennett, S., Demas S., Freeman, G.T., Frischer, B., Oliver, K.B., Peterson, C.A. (2005). Library as place: Rethinking roles, rethinking space. (CLIR Report 129). Retrieved from Council on Library and Information Resources website: http://www.clir.org/pubs/reports/pub129/reports/pub129/contents.html

Carmack, B. (1992). Outline of the building planning process: The players. In R.G. Martin (Ed.), *Libraries for the future: Planning buildings that work* (pp. 25–29). Chicago, IL: American Library Association.

Cohen, A., & Cohen, E. (1979). *Designing and space planning for libraries: A behavioral guide.* New Providence, NJ: R. R. Bowker Co.

Ellsworth, R.E. (1960). *Planning the college and university library building: A book for campus planners and architects.* Boulder, CO: Pruett Press.

Foster, N.F., et al. (2013). *Participatory design of Purdue University's Active Learning Center final report.* (Purdue University Library Report 1). Retrieved from http://docs.lib.purdue.edu/libreports/1

Gibbons, S. & Foster, N.F (2007). Library design and ethnography. In N.F. Foster & S. Gibbons (Eds.) *Studying Students: The Undergraduate Research Project at the University of Rochester* (pp. 20–29). Chicago, IL: Association of College and Research Libraries.

Gerould, J.T. (1932). *The college library building: Its planning and equipment.* New York, NY: C. Scribner's Sons.

Hanley, E.R. (1939). *College and university library buildings.* Chicago, IL: American Library Association.

Healey, E.H. (1991). Planning a library in one week. *American Libraries, 22*(4), 302–304. doi: 10.2307/25632198

Larson, J.F. & Palmer, A.M. (1933). *Architectural planning of the American college.* New York, NY: McGraw-Hill Book Company, Inc.

Martinez, P. (2010, September 1). Engineering library to relocate text volumes and expand digitally. *The Cornell Daily Sun.* Retrieved from http://cornellsun.com/node/43136

Metcalf, K.D. (1965). *Planning academic and research library buildings.* New York, NY: McGraw-Hill Book Company, Inc.

Petroski, H. (2008, September). Moving the books. *Prism.* Retrieved from http://www.prism-magazine.org/sept08/refractions.cfm

Randall, R., Clark, K., Smith, J., & Foster, N.F. (2008). *The next generation of academics: A report on a study conducted at the University of Rochester.* Retrieved from UR Research website: http://hdl.handle.net/1802/6053

Somerville, M.M. & Brown-Sica, M. (2011). Library space planning: A participatory action research approach. *The Electronic Library, 29*(5), 669–681. doi: 10.1108/02640471111177099

Steele, P. & Foster, N.F. (2012). Multidisciplinary rethinking and redesign of library space. Library Assessment Conference: Building effective, sustainable, practical assessment. Charlottesville, VA. Association of Research Libraries. http://libraryassessment.org/bm~doc/Steele_Patricia_2012.pdf.

Steussy, L. (2009, August 29). Budget cuts close physical science and engineering library. *The California Aggie.* Retrieved from http://www.theaggie.org/2009/08/24/budget-cuts-close-physical-science-and-engineering-library/

Twiss-Brooks, A. (2005). A century of progress? Adaptation of the chemistry library at the University of Chicago. *Is-*

sues in Science and Technology, 44 Retrieved from *Issues in Science and Technology* website: http://www.istl.org/05-fall/article1.html

Webb, T.D. (2004). Introduction: Functions and forms. In T.D. Webb (Ed.), *Building libraries for 21st century: The shape of information,* (pp. 5–11). Jefferson, NC: McFarland.

Webster, K. (2010, September). The library space as learning space. *EDUCAUSE Review.* Retrieved from http://www.educause.edu/EDUCAUSE+Review/EDUCAUSEReviewMagazineVolume45/TheLibrarySpaceasLearning-Space/218705

chapter ten. **Study Groups in Libraries: Exponential Benefits**

Alison Bersani, Judi Briden, Sue Cardinal, and Katie Clark

Study groups, those clusters of students scattered around library spaces and obviously working together on something, were a mystery to librarians at the River Campus Libraries in 2010. Our science librarians were familiar with one type of group: formal workshops for engineering and chemistry students that were guided by undergraduates trained to lead them. Yet even in this case, we had little information about how they worked or what they needed. In the social sciences and humanities, we did not have a clue about study groups—did they even exist? So when we decided to refresh our understanding of how undergraduates worked and lived at the University of Rochester, we decided to fill in some of the blanks. We developed a protocol to find out who was in these groups, how the groups formed, and what people in groups were working on. What, we wondered, were the advantages of working together, and what did groups need from the library—if anything.

Team and Group Learning

The University of Rochester has had a formal commitment to group learning since 1995, when Vicki Roth, director of Learning Assistance Services, and Jack Kampmeier, a chemistry professor, introduced a group-learning technique called peer-led team learning (PLTL) to lower-level chemistry courses. The goal of the PLTL workshops was to engage students by requiring them to do group problem solving and discuss the course content with each other and a successful peer leader. Students construct their own understanding of the materials with the help of their fellow students (Gosser et al., 1996). Evaluation of student outcomes over eight years of PLTL in organic chemistry classes showed statistically significant improvements in student performance, retention, and attitudes about the course (Tien, Roth, & Kampmeier, 2002). Since 1995, PLTL has become an integral part of the chemistry and biology curriculum at the University of Rochester.

Of course, the use of group learning predates the University of Rochester's introduction of the team-learning model, and there is an extensive literature discussing the benefits of group learning. By learning in groups, individuals achieve more and learn more (Slavin, 1980 and 1983); they understand the material better as they teach it to each other (Benware & Deci, 1984); they have improved academic performance and have more satisfaction with classes (Lidren & Meier, 1991). Researchers report that, regardless of the subject matter, students working in small groups tend to gain a better understanding of what is taught than when the same content is presented in other instructional formats. Students who work in collaborative groups have more interaction with their fellow students, and therefore grow socially and personally, developing their communication and interpersonal skills. Meanwhile, their academic performance improves, and they become more excited about what they are learning (Whitman, 1988).

Libraries have responded to the increased prevalence of collaborative learning by designing new library spaces to support group work. Much has been written about designing library space to support collaborative learning (O'Farrell & Bates, 2009; Fernekes & Critz, 2010; Gabbard, Kaiser, & Kaunelis, 2007; Kusack, 2002; Bennett, 2007). However, we found no published research looking at study groups who were working in library spaces. Consequently, we decided to conduct this research in our own environment to find out what University of Rochester students do in study groups. We wanted to apply these findings to support the connection between study groups and library resources, facilities, and people.

Research Questions and Methodology

We formed a Study Group sub-team at the start of the Undergraduate Research Refresher Project in the spring of 2010. The librarians who volunteered for this team conducted ethnographic research over the next three semesters to learn about study groups.[1]

Our first task was to identify the information we wanted to gather, and then to narrow this down to those items that might be answered by research we could conduct. At the end of this process, our information needs included—

- What purpose the group served, such as to study or do a project, and the particular course for which it had been formed
- Who formed the group and how they formed it
- Where the group met and why, and whether there were any issues with the space
- When and how frequently the group met
- Who was in the group (for example, the years and majors of the students in the group)
- What the people in the group were working on right then, tools and sources they were using, and people with whom they were in contact
- The students' previous experiences with study groups (A full list of questions appears in Appendix 10A.)

Once we had developed our questions, we decided that the best method for answering them would be to conduct interviews with study groups as they were meeting. We would see the composition of the group, observe the materials and equipment they were using, see the space they were meeting in, and field answers from more than one person. We could also ask them to show us what they had on their computer screens, whiteboards, and notebooks.

Members of our team completed ethics training to receive certification from the University of Rochester's Research Subjects Review Board. This authorized us to enroll research subjects, that is, to provide an information letter about the research and explain their rights as participants. Further preparation for the interviews included arranging for audio and video recorders, purchasing snacks, and scheduling team members to work in pairs. We wanted to interview groups studying for a variety of courses. We chose different library areas in which to solicit participants in the hope that this would enable us to learn about different types of study groups and the spaces that each preferred.

To initiate an interview, two team members approached a likely group as they were working. We briefly explained who we were and that we were interested in learning about study groups and asked whether they were studying the same thing together. Based on their answer, we would request a brief time to ask a few questions, or move on to another likely group. If the group agreed to the interview, we gave each member a copy of the information letter, explained that the interview would be recorded and made sure they understood that they could withdraw from participation at any time. If the interview was audio-recorded, rather than video-recorded, we also took a few photographs to help with our analysis. In planning, we had decided to limit interviews to no more than fifteen minutes. In practice, most interviews were shorter than that. As a thank you, we left a basket of snacks.

Data analysis consisted of viewing and listening to recorded interviews, reading transcripts, viewing photographs, discussing our impressions, comparing answers to questions among the study groups, considering implications of student statements, and writing a report. This chapter is based on all of these, plus further discussions that draw on related findings of other sub-teams doing research for the overall project.

What Is a Study Group?

Before interviewing any groups at all, we had to figure out how to recognize them. Of the many large and small groups working in library spaces, which were the ones we should be talking to? For the purposes of this study, we defined a study group as two or more students who were enrolled in and working on the same course. Study group work always involved discussion of course material. As generous as this definition was, many groups we approached for an interview were simply friends sitting together and working on

different courses—essentially keeping company while working apart. (Find more discussion about these informal study groups in Chapter 4, "Picture My Work.")

Study Spaces and Groups

We interviewed seven study groups during 2010 and 2011 in two campus libraries, the Gleason Library and the Carlson Science and Engineering Library. This section summarizes information about the locations and each of the groups we interviewed.

Gleason Library

In the main library building centrally located on campus and open around-the-clock during the semester, Gleason Library was designed to accommodate both collaborative and individual work. There are no books and no staffed service points. It is close to dorms and convenient to food and drink. With large open spaces on a single floor, natural lighting, and movable furni-

Figure 10.1. Gleason Library (Photo by Jan Regan Photography)

Figure 10.2. Studio in Gleason Library (Photo by Jan Regan Photography)

Figure 10.3. Group working in Gleason Library (Photo by Jan Regan Photography)

ture, Gleason offers a mix of comfortable seating, small café tables, large tables, individual study spaces, and group cubicles and studios. The noise levels range from low in off hours to high during peak use. Students demonstrate ownership of the space and know they contributed to its design. It is the most popular study space on campus.

We interviewed four study groups in Gleason Library. The first was a group of three first-year students taking an introductory biology class, studying in a cubicle. The second, also in a cubicle, comprised a sophomore, two juniors, and a senior working on a group presentation for an introductory marketing class.

The third group—two sophomores taking an engineering course—was sitting at a cafe table studying together for an exam. The fourth was a group of four graduate students from the business school, working on weekly case studies for a finance course.

Carlson Science and Engineering Library

Located on the south side of campus among a cluster of science buildings, Carlson Library has study spaces on all three floors but offers designated group study areas on the first and third levels. There are two enclosed group study rooms. The large spaces are open, light, and airy with furniture that is less portable than in Gleason but not completely fixed. Students feel free to talk as groups but tend to keep the noise levels down.

We interviewed three study groups in Carlson Library. The first comprised three students taking a 200-level biology course, studying for an exam on the third floor. The second, on the first floor, was larger: six first-year students taking an introductory chemistry course, working on a lab report.

The third group was meeting in a first-floor study room and was larger still: nine first-year students taking an introductory chemistry course, working on a workshop assignment.

Figure 10.4. Group study room in Carlson Library

Figure 10.5. First-floor group study area in Carlson Library

Figure 10.6. Third-floor group study area in Carlson Library

Insights on Groups and Group Work

Our analyzed data point to several characteristics of group work that seem to hold across the many groups we interviewed. These insights have to do with the formation of groups, the activities in which they are engaged, and especially in the ways they support the learning of the individuals who participate in them.

How Groups Formed and Met

The study groups we interviewed were either assigned by the professor or organized independently by the students in the group. When assigned by the professor, in a business class for example, the group had a presentation or assignment to complete. For other courses, such as biology and engineering, students formed study groups on their own. Most of these groups were open to anyone from the class who wanted to join.

One group of biology students that we interviewed coordinated their meetings before and after tests by texting each other. Another group of engineering students gathered at tables in a highly trafficked area in Gleason Library and simply waited for their classmates to walk by and join them. This informal study group came together weekly on the night before their homework assignment was due.

We might text each other and say, "You want to go work on this?" But there'll be other people here, too.—Engineering student interviewed in Gleason Library

What Groups Were Doing

In general, the groups we met were reading; writing in notebooks and on laptops; listening as a group and talking and listening to each other; writing on whiteboards; looking things up online for assignments in Blackboard or on textbook websites and using Google; doing homework; socializing or taking a break; and sharing files and notes. They often consulted their course pages,

lecture notes, textbooks, and materials suggested by the professor or teaching assistant.

How Groups Supported Individual Work

As students enter college, they discover that there is much more material to learn than in high school and that they have to manage their own time. When asked why they formed a study group, the students we interviewed generally replied that the work was "hard."

Our analysis of the interview transcripts suggests that working in groups supports individual learning by—

- Helping students collaborate on the background preparation for assignments
- Leveraging social influence to focus on studies
- Enabling students to share information and fill in knowledge gaps
- Giving students an opportunity to discuss content and concepts and to master course material by teaching it to others in the group

Five of the groups we interviewed engaged in individual learning and individual project work. In these groups, each person needed to complete an assignment or exam on his or her own.

I mean, you can't type up the same report, but you can talk about the ideas and then make it your own. You can't have the same document.
—Biology student interviewed in Gleason Library

Well, we cannot really divide up the work, because each of us have to understand the material in order to learn. So if you divided the load, we can read the summary, but then for this class summary doesn't... you need to know it.—Biology student interviewed in Carlson Library

Students worked together to share their knowledge and provided emotional and social support. Just being together helped students focus on their studies.

> *I mean, the other people in the group are just, like, a resource to you. And it's easier to, like, stay focused I guess, if there are two other people doing the same work as you.*—Biology student interviewed in Gleason Library

Studying with others could fill in knowledge gaps. The group knew more than the individual and when all shared what they knew, the individual was more informed. The students we interviewed who were studying for biology exams had all been present at the lectures, but some absorbed or recorded information more clearly and accurately than others. In a group setting, they could share their insights with each other when needed.

> *Like, I would miss something from a lecture, and then I would ask her what did he say about this slide or that slide and then they will know.*—Biology student interviewed in Gleason Library

> *It is helpful, because it helps you organize the material for the test, like if you don't know something, someone else can answer it. And if someone else doesn't know something that you know, it's a helpful way of studying. Especially for a big test or final.*—Chemistry student interviewed in Carlson Library

Students were able to discuss concepts with others who shared similar language and experiences, until they "got it." Chemistry workshop students worked together on problems. They talked as they work, and group members gave each other feedback on whether or not they were expressing newly learned concepts correctly and completely. This exemplifies Tien's "community of learners" (Tien et al., 2002).

> *So, we all talk about it while we're doing the sections, and then, like, when we're talking about—it's easier to talk through studying, I guess. But then, like, you would do memorization on your own.*—Biology student interviewed in Gleason Library

Some students learned the materials faster than others and were able to rephrase the information in language that other students related to and could understand. Teaching reinforces what an expert student knows. In one case, engineering students were all working on the same problem set. Each student worked independently until a stuck student asked another expert student for help. The expert student showed the stuck student how to do the problem.

> *But when there's a problem, if you don't know how to do it, somebody can show you and it helps both of you.*—Engineering student interviewed in Gleason Library

How Groups Supported Team Work

Some groups were formed by the professor to work together for the entire course or just to complete a specific assignment. In addition to the course concepts, students learned how to be part of a team, divide up a large project, and synthesize work from several sources to complete a project.

> *No, we assign to each person; the question we have to complete ourselves and then one person will combine all of the answers together and then hand it to the professor.*—Business school student in Gleason Library

Students also told us that working as a group helped to compensate for individual limitations and split up the workload, making it lighter for any one person. They said that group dynamics were very important; teams that worked well together did better than when individuals in the team could not cooperate effectively. Depending on the grade for the assignment, having the entire group receive a single grade could be a benefit or a drawback, especially if team members did not contribute equally. One student mentioned a problem in an earlier group with a student who never participated but still got credit.

Variations in Group Preferences

The libraries provide a variety of spaces to accommodate the varying preferences and practices of students doing academic work. Flexible seating, large and small tables, individual desks, computer seating, and moveable furniture all help to meet the needs of individual students and groups. What really surprised us in this research was the wide variation in study group preferences regarding noise level and the number of people present and moving around near the group study space. Conditions that were perfect for one study group were entirely wrong for another. Flexibility of space is a key asset.

Despite the high noise level and appearance of chaos, several of the groups we interviewed preferred to meet in the Gleason Library. It did not seem to us as librarians to be conducive to serious studying at all. The engineering students we interviewed in Gleason liked to meet there because it was a high-traffic area, making it easy to see and be seen by classmates. Other groups mentioned that Gleason was noisy, but since people were generally discussing homework it was an acceptable type of noise. As long as it was "scholarly noise," it was deemed conducive to studying.

It's a library, but it's not 100% quiet, so we can feel free to talk to each other about what we're doing. And you can write on any of these walls. That's why we like the cubicle, because, like, we're contained—people can't really hear our conversation as much—and we can write on the walls.—Biology student in Gleason Library

Some students use headphones or earplugs to adapt to their surroundings. One student was wearing headphones while working in his group and when asked what he was listening to, he responded:

Usually music so I can drown out everything.— Engineering student in Gleason Library

One group of students in a biology class deliberately chose the third floor of the Carlson Library. This quiet, out-of-the-way space would not have worked for the engineering students, but for this group it was ideal. Talking was acceptable, but the atmosphere was still quiet. When asked why they were studying in Carlson, as opposed to Gleason, they responded:

It's quieter than Gleason, it's better than Gleason, I would say. It's quiet and everyone respects each other. Like, we don't giggle, laugh, scream, you know.—Biology student in Carlson Library

A student in another group mentioned,

I've studied a lot with groups in Carlson for bio and chem sometimes. I like Carlson because it's medium—Rush Rhees is quiet and Gleason's loud… yeah, Gleason's like, if you want to procrastinate and kind of do your work, you go there.—Chemistry student in Carlson Library

Why the Library

We wanted to know why students chose to meet and study in the library rather than in empty classrooms, business school study rooms, dorm rooms, or a campus coffee shop. One reason was that the libraries are available more hours than most other spaces. During the semester, Carlson Library is open from 8:00 a.m. until 2:00 a.m. most days, and Gleason Library does not close at all. This makes it possible to find a space whenever a group wants to meet. In contrast, empty classrooms are closed after hours to secure classroom technology. Study rooms in the business school require reservations at least 24 hours in advance, are often booked up, and are only available to business school students (Simon Graduate School of Business, 2011).

The proximity to academic buildings comes into play as well. Carlson Library is near a cluster of science buildings, and one group mentioned that they studied in Carlson because they were already on that side of campus for classes.

When asked why they had chosen the library over more social spots, such as dorm rooms and campus coffee shops, we learned that avoiding distractions is a key objective. A dorm room is full of personal to-dos as well as fun activities, and a coffee shop is more of a social place where people feel free to chat, interrupt, and spend time standing in line buying food and drinks.

We need the atmosphere here, so we can concentrate on studying, because in my room, I will [do] some other things and not concentrate."—Business school student interviewed in Gleason Library

Yeah, because other students [in Gleason], I think they are also discussing homework, but in Starbucks and Wilson Commons most of the people are eating food and chatting.—Business school student in Gleason Library

One student mentioned that she was embarrassed to be caught on Facebook in the library, so she was better able to focus on her work while there. Even in the library, some groups preferred spaces with solid or modular walls to cut down on noise and visual distractions, mainly other people talking or walking by.

Access to Reserve Books

Before starting this research, we assumed that some study groups chose to meet in an area because it was close to the books available on reserve in the library. Contrary to our expectations, reserve books were mentioned as a draw for only one of the seven study groups that we interviewed. When asked why they were in the Carlson Library instead of Gleason, a student in the group responded:

Student: *Because they have the book on reserve here.*

Interviewer: *The book on reserve. And do you own the textbook yourself?*

Student: *I do. We share a book, but I don't carry it around campus.... It's really heavy. We don't like to carry it around.*—Biology student in Carlson Library

In one other interview, a student mentioned using textbooks from library reserve, however, not for use in a study group. We still have questions about the value to study groups of proximity to reserve materials.

Other Aspects of Group Work

Our work raised questions that had not been part of our original inquiry or about which we had known very little at the beginning of the study, such as the use of Facebook in connection with group study.

Do students engage in study group-like behavior online? When we look at the freshman Facebook group, some of the conversation looks a lot like what goes on in a traditional study group. Within their first few weeks of arriving on campus, students are turning to their peers for help. For some of our freshmen, their University of Rochester Facebook page functions as an *ad hoc* study group. Facebook does not always support a face-to-face group, but it does provide a way to get assistance from other students enrolled in the same classes. There were many occasions on which freshmen turned to Facebook when they needed an answer to a homework assignment. A stuck student asked for help on a certain problem in a certain class. Another expert student responded with information about how to get the answer. There were some students who used Facebook to set up actual study groups that would meet later, face to face. Facebook may be another way that students turn to their peers for help in filling in the gaps of their own knowledge.

The Library's Role in Supporting Study Groups

When we began this research, we had no doubt about the importance of library support for study groups. By our reasoning, libraries must be involved in the teaching and learning mission of the University, and this includes study groups. One component is working directly with study groups, but another important element is working with faculty who incorporate group work in library spaces as part of their teaching activities. By providing well focused support, we strengthen our library's association with students and faculty. Even as digital resources, remote access, and Internet search engines raise questions about the library's continued relevance, we seek to better understand what it is that students need to do and the ways in which the library is uniquely positioned to aid them.

Although undergraduate education is in flux, we see more and more support for experiential and team-based learning. We will be in a better position to support new team-based activities if we have built a solid foundation of support for existing study group behavior.

Encouraging study groups to meet in the library increases the opportunity to interact with students and promote library resources. Furthermore, we believe we can engage less formally with study groups in the library than with students in the classroom, and this informal

engagement provides greater opportunity for understanding the culture of a class from the students' perspective, including learning more about their skills and the tools that they use.

Libraries can encourage and support study groups by providing the best study spaces on campus. We know that students prefer the library for its studious atmosphere and count on being able to accomplish work there. As library use becomes more about spaces rather than access to traditional resources, gathering feedback from students is crucial to developing and maintaining future spaces. From our observations, the most important attributes of great group study spaces are good lighting, comfortable temperatures, large tables and chairs, and easily accessible whiteboards. Students also want wireless Internet access and electrical outlets to support their laptops and mobile devices. It is helpful if food is allowed and conveniently available. Students need to feel that they can talk without disrupting others and that they can hear each other. Additionally, the best space is easily accessible and preferably located near classrooms.

One group was drawn to the Gleason Library because of the large windows. The view was nice and the natural lighting was great.

Student: *Actually, that window is fabulous, so we saw it [the library].*

Interviewer: *The window... so you saw it [the library] through the window?*

Student: *Yeah, the first time I went to climb up the stairs and check out how we could look from here, and it was fantastic, so after that, this group liked to sit here.*—Business school student in Gleason Library

Temperatures matter, as well. This same group said they would not study in the business school rooms because the rooms were too cold.

Figure 10.7. Group work in Carlson Library's third-floor group study area

In a different group, people mentioned that another room in the library was too warm.

We observed that students needed large tables to spread out their laptops, textbooks, notes, printouts, phones, food, and drinks. The students mentioned that some tables wobbled, so sturdiness is important, too.

Whiteboards consistently came up as crucial to group work to promote the spontaneous sharing of ideas as well as providing mental and physical barriers. Even in a public area, a mobile whiteboard can create a feeling of having private space.

We asked several groups whether they would use a projector connected to a laptop for sharing notes and ideas. This was perceived as too formal. They preferred whiteboards, which seemed to encourage spontaneous collaboration. Students noted:

We share notes. So we had it written down, but it was nice for everyone to see what was going on at the same time.—Chemistry student interviewed in Carlson Library

And if there's just a table and no whiteboard, then it's really hard to communicate with everybody, because it'll just be one person talking and no one can really see them. So it's easier if you have a board to present on.—Chemistry student interviewed in Carlson Library

It is important that the library support the technology that students use. Several groups mentioned the need for additional outlets and better wireless coverage. These issues came up, for example, when we asked why one group was meeting in the library rather than another space on campus:

Figure 10.8. Whiteboards used to create "private space" in Gleason Library

I don't know where else we would get a big table with wireless.—Biology major in Carlson Library

Allowing food creates a more comfortable atmosphere for studying. Some groups kept long hours, sometimes studying late into the night, and needed food for breaks and just to keep going. This does not mean that cafés make great study spaces for all students; many find it impossible to work well in the hubbub of purely social spaces.

Acting on Our Findings

Based on what we have learned, we are building upon our existing support for study groups in the River Campus Libraries. We continue to ensure that our spaces can support group work by providing a variety of tables, chairs, good lighting, wireless, electrical outlets, and whiteboards. Students need to be able to talk, be near

food, continue to work late into the night, and find spaces that accommodate different levels of noise and traffic.

Although students did not request more computers, separate rooms, roving librarians, projectors, screens, or spaces that can be reserved, we continue to monitor whether any of these develop as identifiable needs for our students. As our library strategic planning begins to focus on support for experiential learning and innovation spaces, items on this list, along with others that we have not yet identified, may assume greater importance.

One group we interviewed checked out textbooks to use when studying, and we want to learn more about the desirability of making textbooks from the library easier to borrow. Therefore, our Physics-Optics-Astronomy Library recently instituted an open textbook collection. Originally intended for use by teaching assistants meeting with students in the library, this collection of print textbooks and solution manuals is now available on open shelves in the library, without the need for staff intervention. The materials are heavily used by both students and teaching assistants, and there is evidence that some of the use is by students working in groups. The success of this effort will lead to experiments with open access to textbooks in other disciplines. We also want to investigate whether online textbooks would be attractive to study groups and, if so, how the library might address that need.

We heard in our interviews that groups sometimes have trouble finding a good place to study. Could a "find a space" app help them locate an available space more easily or allow them to join another group already meeting? We are currently investigating whether the GroupFinder application developed by North Carolina State University Libraries can be adapted for use in our environment.[2]

We plan to build on the library's reputation as a place where scholarly work is done, perhaps through a marketing campaign. This could help study groups and individual students discover sooner the benefits of using library spaces for doing serious work.

We also hope to expand our research to investigate study groups that meet outside of the library and those that are organized around courses in other disciplines. In the current study we were not able to schedule interviews with groups in either of these categories and hope to fill this gap in a future study. This will help us extend the benefits of library support to even more students.

When librarians at the University of Rochester's River Campus Libraries decided to learn more about study groups, we had little concrete information about how they worked and what they needed from the library. Although our findings are not startling, in the aggregate we have built a solid picture of variations among study groups, and we have identified shared needs. We know that some groups are formed to meet the requirements for some courses and that other study groups are organized independently by the

students taking a course. Our interviews have revealed that study groups have preferences for where, when, and under what conditions they work, just as individuals do. If we had any notion before undertaking this research that the needs of study groups would be generic, we do not think that now. We have a better understanding of which aspects of the library are important to the functions of study groups and are taking steps to improve our support. By providing a variety of spaces with adequate lighting, different seating options, and whiteboards, we can support the basic functions of study groups and encourage important peer teaching opportunities. At the same time, we know that group work is receiving greater emphasis in higher education. Based on our understanding of more traditional study groups, the library will be well situated to identify and address the emerging needs of groups engaged in experiential learning and innovation. Now that we "have a clue" about our study groups in the River Campus Libraries, we fully expect to support their future needs in new learning landscapes.

Appendix 10A. Script and Questions for Interviewing Study Groups

We work in the library and are doing interviews to find out what study groups do and what they need from the library. We'd like to ask you some questions. We won't take more than 15 minutes of your time.

1. What course is this group for? What years are you and what are your majors?

2. Does the group have a name?

3. Did you get assigned to this study group or did you form it by yourselves? How did this group form? Have you had the same people each time or have the people changed? Is everyone physically in the same place?

4. Where has this group met the last few times? How often have you met? Do you ever work overnight?

5. Why are you meeting in this place? What are the benefits and drawbacks of this location? Does it get too noisy anytime?

6. Do you contend for meeting space with other groups? What do you do if your space is taken?

7. What are you working on today? Have you used any resources, such as notes, books or articles (paper or online), websites, other? How did you know these resources existed and how did you get them? Can you show us? Do you need to do much printing?

8. Have you consulted any experts, such as a professor, TA, someone who works in the library?

9. Are you using music in your study group? Have you ever? How?

10. Have any of you been in a study group before? Can you tell us a little about those experiences? Did you work in a study group in high school or was college the first time? How are high school and college study groups alike and different?

11. What is the best thing about a study group? What doesn't work about a study group? What can you do in a study group that you can't do or that is hard to do alone? What is better done alone?

12. Have you learned anything in your study group that you use when you are working on your own?

13. Have you worked with the same people in more than one group?

14. Are study groups better for certain subjects?

15. Do you share information through e-mail, Facebook, Google Docs, Twitter, etc.?

Notes

1. Team members were Barbara Alvarez, Alison Bersani, Judi Briden, Sue Cardinal, and Katie Clark.
2. For more information about GroupFinder, visit http://www.lib.ncsu.edu/dli/projects/groupfinder

References

Bennett, S. (2007). First questions for designing higher education learning spaces, *The Journal of Academic Librarianship, 33*(1), 14–26. doi:10.1016/j.acalib.2006.08.015

Benware, C.A. & Deci, E.L. (1984). Quality of learning with an active versus passive motivational set. *American Educational Research Journal, 21*(4), 755–765. doi: 10.2307/1162999

Fernekes, B. and Critz, L.J.O. (2010). Collaborative learning and convergence: Library strategies and solutions with an eye on the USG Information Technology Strategic Plan. *Georgia Library Quarterly, 47*(4), 5–11. Retrieved from digitalcommons.kennesaw.edu/glq/vol47/iss4/3/

Gabbard, R.B., Kaiser, A., & Kaunelis, D. (2007). Redesigning a Library Space for Collaborative Learning. *Computer in Libraries, 27*(5), 6–11. Retrieved from http://www.infotoday.com/cilmag/may07/index.shtml

Gosser, D., Roth, V., Gafney, L., Kampmeier, J., Strozak, V., Varma-Nelson, P., Radel, S., & Weiner, M. (1996). Workshop chemistry: Overcoming the barriers to student success. *The Chemical Educator, 1*(1), 1–17. doi: 10.1333/s00897960002a

Kusack, J.M. (2002). Fostering collaborative learning and group work in libraries. *Library Administration & Management, 16*(2), 79–82. Retrieved from OmniFile Full Text Mega (H.W. Wilson). (Accession Number 502878207)

Lidren, D.M., Meier, S.E., & Brigham, T.A. (1991). The effects of minimal and maximal peer tutoring systems on the academic performance of college. *Psychological Record, 41*(1), 69–77. Retrieved from http://psycnet.apa.org/psycinfo/1991-19749-001

O'Farrell, M. and Bates, J. (2009). Student information behaviors during group projects. *Aslib Proceedings, 61*(3), 302–315. doi: 10.1108/00012530910959835

Simon Graduate School of Business. (2011). *Student Handbook, 2011–2012.* Rochester, NY: University of Rochester. Retrieved from http://www.simon.rochester.edu/why-choose-simon/registrar/index.aspx

Slavin, R.E. (1980). Cooperative learning. *Review of Educational Research, 50*(2), 315–342. doi: 10.3102/00346543050002315

Slavin, R.E. (1983). When does cooperative learning increase student achievement? *Psychological Bulletin, 94*(3), 429–445. doi:10.1037/0033-2909.94.3.429

Tien, L.T., Roth, V., & Kampmeier, J.A. (2002). Implementation of a peer-led team learning instructional approach in an undergraduate organic chemistry course. *Journal of Research in Science Teaching, 39*, 606–632. doi:10.1002/tea.10038

Whitman, N.A. & Fife, J.D. (1988). *Peer teaching: To teach is to learn twice.* (ASHE-ERIC Higher Education Report No. 4.) Retrieved from http://eric.ed.gov/?id=ED305016

chapter eleven. **Where Do We Go from Here?**

Solomon Blaylock, Judi Briden, and LeRoy LaFleur

In his 1973 dissertation, Douglas Zweizig notes that one common and persistent limitation of library and information science research is that "researchers have examined the user from the perspective of the library. In effect," he states, "they have looked at the user in the life of the library rather than the library in the life of the user" (p. 15). Throughout our efforts to better understand the students at the University of Rochester, we have worked to maintain a focus on the life of the user, and indeed we have learned a great deal about undergraduate life on campus and the ways in which students work, study, play, and develop as scholars. As reflective observers, however, our research also leads us to look for deeper meaning in our findings, particularly with reference to the role of the library in the lives of these students, now and in the future. What are the implications of this research on the student research process, library practice, and faculty as intermediaries between the two? In this chapter we offer a few ideas on where we might go from here by highlighting some of the more notable implications of our research and how they affect the work we do in the library.

Implications for Students

In the early 1960s Pierre Bourdieu, Alain Darbel, and Dominique Schnapper undertook their now famous study of the cultural attitudes of European museumgoers (Bourdieu, Darbel, & Schnapper, 1990). They discovered that for much of the public a museum was something of a sacred space—a place in which special rules applied, certain attitudes were appropriately effected, and

behavior was necessarily modified. In a similar way, we wondered what the recorded comments of undergraduates might reveal about their ideas of the library as an institution. We turned our attention back to the interview transcripts with an eye toward any mention of the library and, specifically, comments that suggested *identities* that the library had assumed for students. We wanted to know what students think an academic library *is* and what it is *for*.

Interestingly, during the course of the interviews we conducted, many students expressed little need for traditional library services or physical collections. This attitude appears to be a manifestation of a growing trend among undergraduates generally (Asher, Duke, & Green, 2010; Head & Eisenberg, 2011, p. 3), and yet the River Campus Libraries continue to be centers of constant student activity. If students are not at the library to search the stacks or to seek assistance from reference librarians, just why are they here?

It seems that undergraduates flock to the library to study because they see it as "the right place" to study. That is to say, they find the library environment conducive to academic work by virtue of its "studious atmosphere" and the many physical and social resources it offers. The library's continued relevance to undergraduates is thus both practical and ideational. It is a relevance that we believe can and should be maintained and enhanced. Toward that end, it seems wise to play to our established strengths while being vigilant to develop new ones in light of evolving needs and service models.

The Library Atmosphere

When asked why she chooses the library over other places to study, one of the students interviewed by the Study Group sub-team replied: "We need the atmosphere here so we can concentrate on studying ... In my room I will [do] other things and not concentrate." It is clear that this "atmosphere" looms large in the library's identity for students, but explaining just what it consists of conceptually is tricky. Student comments seem to indicate that it may be as simple as having access to necessary physical resources in a non-distracting environment, one in which their presence is a sign to friends that they are engaged in serious study. More pointedly, it may signify a sort of institutional cachet distinguishing the library as a place for serious research. This sober, dignified image is of special interest as it somewhat complicates the relationship between student and library. On the one hand, it ensures the library's importance for undergraduates as a dedicated space for academic work, and on the other, it may contribute to feelings of intimidation that prevent students from connecting with such perceived authority figures as reference librarians. By simultaneously celebrating the library as a venerable institution of scholarship and actively working to break down communication barriers between students, faculty, and library staff, we believe the library can contribute much to the personal growth and academic maturity so vital to the success of undergraduates. How these goals should be pursued will differ for various institutions. It will be necessary to bring to bear the ideas and efforts not only of reference librarians, but of library staff and library administration as well.

Engaging in research of the sort pursued by the Undergraduate Research Refresher team at our institution is itself an important way in which a meaningful and mutually beneficial relationship between students and the library may be forged and sustained. A number of the students interviewed expressed surprise and delight that the library was actively engaged with undergraduates in order to understand their needs and challenges and support them more effectively. One survey we administered via iPad to students in the library elicited several positive comments regarding the library's use of new technology in this way. A recent study of undergraduate technology use at the University of Rochester strongly indicated that students prefer to keep their social networking and academic spheres separate. Still, a large number also indicated that blogging, chat, and other technologies enhance their learning experience (Fredericksen, 2012). We believe that when we use up-to-date technical resources skillfully, students perceive the library as an ever-relevant, evolving support system for their academic work. Doubtless many more ways in which to connect with students will present themselves to attentive library staff.

Physical Resources

Time and again in their interviews, students told us that they need wireless Internet, electrical outlets, bright lighting, comfortable furniture, whiteboards, semi-private study spaces, computers, printers, tables, photocopiers, and other physical resources for their work as individuals and in groups. Students also expressed the need for a variety of environments to facilitate effective study in changing sets of circumstances, for example, alone or in a group, quiet or a little noisy, brightly or dimly lit, or in privacy or surrounded by people. Each scenario carried with it a set of physical requirements relating to lighting, temperature, distractions, and so on. Undergraduates, working increasingly in groups, make heavy use of semi-private spaces and whiteboards, while, interestingly, we rarely observe our several wall mounted plug-and-play screens in use. We must maintain regular contact with the student body to track their changing needs and make sure that researchers, administration, and library staff cooperate to deliver required resources. Some might object that making physical resources an area of intense focus detracts from the "real work" of the library, but we disagree. As Dr. Jason Martin of University of Central Florida Libraries has observed, "In order for students to come to the library, librarians need to give them what they want and need. Simply holding on to the belief that students will come to the library because it is there not only is unhelpful but also can present a danger to the future and vitality of the profession"(Martin, 2008, p. 74).

Not all student interview comments regarding the libraries' physical resources were positive. Some expressed frustration with the perceived labyrinthine layout of the largest of the River Campus Libraries, while others complained of spotty wireless Internet access and a lack of electrical outlets. This does not surprise us as we found laptop use to be ubiquitous among undergrads in the library. Undergraduates generally view wireless networking as a basic utility service, one that they expect to be able to use while studying anywhere in the library. The library can proactively address these concerns and thereby distinguish itself as a place dedicated to study and committed to making academic work as convenient as possible.

Social Resources

In 2005, Elizabeth Stephan at the University of Mississippi Libraries noted: "More and more, academic libraries are moving toward being community centers as well as research centers" (p. 3). This has only proven truer in the years since. A number of University of Rochester undergraduates with whom we spoke mentioned the benefits of working among their fellow students at the library. The library environment continues to prove especially conducive to group study, which we have seen to be an increasingly frequent choice for successful undergraduates. One might be tempted to assume that students are always looking for peace and quiet when they choose to study at the library, but we have found that often, particularly in the case of group study, something like the opposite is the case. As one biology student observed, "It's a library, but it's not 100% quiet, so we can feel free to talk to each other about what we're doing." Undergrads also noted that being surrounded by working fellow students discourages frivolous activity. "I feel like if you're on Facebook, and other people are just studying, you will feel embarrassed to be on Facebook," one student commented. It seems important, therefore, to ensure that there are spaces in the library set aside to accommodate a number of different study styles and scenarios, all well equipped with the kinds of resources previously outlined and accessible late at night or even available around the clock.

Challenges

Meeting the academic needs of students is a preeminent concern for university libraries, and the manner in which that goal is approached will naturally change as the student body does. Regular and direct communication with the students themselves will be key in keeping our focus sharp and our concerns relevant. But undergraduates, especially freshmen, often have academic needs they themselves are not yet able to identify or communicate. It therefore becomes important to consider how we as library professionals and staff members can effectively anticipate student needs and offer assistance proactively. We need to find ways to engage students directly and help them understand where they need assistance. Part of this process could involve fostering relationships among undergraduates, faculty members, and graduate students in their chosen disciplines. Chapters 5, 6, and 7 argue the importance of these relationships to an undergraduate's eventual success, and we believe the library can play an important role in initiating and nurturing these important relationships, for example, by sponsoring formal and informal events that bring these groups—which do not typically mix socially—together. Another part of helping students with their academic work is simply to do what we have been doing—help students navigate our collections and databases in order to uncover what Andrew Abbott calls the "plenitude of interpretations" they need to gain a broad understanding of their topic of current concern (p. 538; see Chapter 7, "Research as Connection").

How do we go about meeting these goals in practical terms? How do we stay up to date on trends in publishing, technology, communication, and, in particular, on the trends among the students we serve? How do we address the financial issues that arise as we consider expanded service offerings and other expensive propositions? The energy with which we pursue the answers to those questions—questions that will need answering over and over again as the years pass—will be a direct investment in the future of the library and the future academic success of our undergrads.

Implications for Library Staff

We have observed that the library is in a unique position to foster formal and informal interactions that support student learning, skill development, maturation, and, ultimately, success. It is already a favorite place for students for studying, working, and meeting with friends. We now consider a few ideas for student-focused activities and programming suggested by the research reported in this book and briefly reflect on what these ideas might mean for library staff.

Host activities to highlight positive role models for students. While students have opportunities to interact with faculty in the classroom, fewer informal and non-curricular opportunities are available. The library is in a position to increase opportunities for students to encounter those who might serve as role models in ways that are not tied to course expectations. What might that look like? Activities could include "research storytelling" by faculty, graduate students, or upper-level undergraduates. A successful researcher might describe some defining element in his or her evolution from a novice to an expert. Experts may also be library and campus staff with individual stories to tell. Another opportunity for librarians could involve coaching students individually, apart from formal instruction—essentially informal modeling with examples of personal practice and experience. The library could explore the concept of personal librarians, collaborate with residential advisors on programming to strengthen subject liaison relationships with students, or encourage and support librarians who want to become academic advisors. Indeed a number of librarians at the University of Rochester are already serving as advisors for incoming freshman. Many opportunities exist beyond the scope of formal instruction programs. For these efforts to be successful, the library will need to invest in ongoing staff education, maintain engaged staff in sufficient numbers, and make staff available to students for more hours of the day.

Seek ways to associate the library with a personal passion. Library programming can encourage "finding your passion at the library" as a way to learn more about library resources in an area of strong interest and, in the process, to acquire useful research skills. We should consider targeting the interests of individuals and groups who may not otherwise spend much time in the library and look for other avenues to embed research into the pursuit of personal intellectual interests. In the process, library staff will likely learn much from their passionate students; there are many ideas and useful sources that students will bring to the conversation.

Understand that students exhibit different types and stages of maturity at any particular point. For library staff, awareness of various kinds and differing rates of maturity may help in working more effectively with students, who are often in mid-stream on one level or another. By simply keeping this possibility in mind, staff may be more flexible and recognize sooner any issues that might be related to levels of maturity. Importantly, if library staff members are to focus intentionally on students as maturing individuals, they will require awareness of and access to campus support services for students who are struggling.

Advise on choosing tools and developing skill in the use of tools. With the explosion of new tools library staff may question how they can keep up. Even familiar tools change frequently and require maintenance learning. One approach to address these issues is to pursue a program of learning collaboratively with others in the academic community and to share the development of expertise more broadly. Collaboration would distribute the "cost" of keeping current and strengthen ties across the institution. This implies that making their expertise available is not the only service that library staff might offer. A rich learning environment in which staff members are participants and learners alongside students and faculty creates additional opportunities for productive interaction.

Re-examine the formal elements of library instruction in light of the widespread use of the "whatever works" approach to doing research. One approach would be to emphasize the value of an iterative process when doing research, a process that may be idiosyncratic. Through iteration, competence is developed beyond the immediate goal of finding sources for a specific assignment. Expertise is built over time across assignments and projects, and time spent doing research has intrinsic value outside of a particular assignment. Using a "whatever works" approach still leaves room for learning additional strategies through formal instruction and informal coaching.

Consider "ad campaigns" highlighting findings from ethnographic research. Some possibilities from our research include—

- "Ten Habits of Highly Effective Students"— brief descriptions of the practices of successful students. This concept developed from a brainstorming session among library staff who were involved in conducting our research. (See Appendix 11A for a list of 26 qualities that appeared repeatedly in our research as markers of successful student behavior.)
- "Advice" spots from seniors to younger students, such as "Something I wish I'd discovered sooner"
- Highlighting the peer-reviewed, scholarly qualities of library content
- Associating the library with personal passion (discussed in a previous section)

Any of these campaigns might be developed using established communication pathways or they might be viewed as an opportunity to experiment with new media.

Show off the library's latest technologies. Our students were impressed when surveyed in the library by staff using an iPad, and the discussion that ensued about the technology provided opportunity for further dialogue. But technologies change quickly and so do ideas about how to use them effectively to engage students. Deciding which technologies to focus on and how many resources to invest in can be difficult. Having staff who are willing experimenters helps, but care should be taken to balance investment and expected return. As academic libraries develop spaces for experiential learning and innovative technologies, staff will need to develop new "muscles" to support these initiatives. As time goes by, our students and faculty may engage in much less "subdued interaction" and much more group work in the library. Staff will need to understand different types of learning experiences and the activities they engender. Team-based and game-based assignments and some creative endeavors may be much more active and social, possibly even drawing in passersby. Some library staff might become more involved as participants and contributors, rather than only as facilitators. How compatible will this new, potentially noisy and active learning be with the highly valued scholarly atmosphere that our students currently seek out? What can we do as library staff to help both needs coexist productively within our spaces? None of this is clearly mapped territory; comfort with uncertainty, along with a sense of adventure, will be an asset for staff as they adapt to changing roles in a changing environment. At the same time, such changes will offer significant opportunities for further ethnographic and user research, with a view to understanding anew how people are doing their work and how libraries can best support and contribute to their efforts.

Implications for Faculty

Faculty members play a unique role in determining the way students experience research as well as how they relate to librarians and library staff. Ideally, students learn to see themselves as an integral part of the community of researchers supported by the libraries and the University. Since classroom faculty are a primary means through which undergraduate students learn about library services, library staff should make sure to inform faculty members about services, technology, and resources so that faculty can pass this information on to students. Of course, this will also ensure that faculty themselves are able to take full advantage of everything the library has to offer.

We noted during our interviews with faculty that many provide students with resources for research or make specific recommendations for resources students should consult as part of their work. While this strategy is clearly in line with the instructional mission that faculty pursue in their courses, it may serve to discourage some students from seeking out resources independently through the library. Raising faculty awareness of this concern is one way we can use the results of our ethnographic studies to enhance the research practices of students. A number of faculty members admitted to us that they do not know how their students go about finding resources, which would seem to indicate that the manner in which students find information is often not a specific concern for faculty. Our research on faculty expectations bears out that students produce the most successful papers when they take on topics that interest them, which naturally leads to fuller engagement. Librarians can work with students to identify and select these kinds of topics, but faculty obviously play the central role. Students often see a professor as the sole authority in determining the success of their research endeavors, but faculty can help extend this credibility to librarians and library staff members whom they trust. Furthermore, our research indicates that undergraduates will see clear benefits in working with librarians whose instruction strategies and approaches to research are in sync with those of their professors, so it behooves librarians to work closely with faculty to understand their expectations regarding student assignments and research practices. Faculty members who are open to such an expanded role for librarians—as partners in designing curriculum and experiences for students—will see their students develop more effectively as researchers.

Different subjects and disciplines require that students use the library and utilize library spaces in different ways. Faculty members are already aware of this, as experts in their respective disciplines, but undergraduate students are typically novice researchers and require extra help from library staff, particularly if instructors are not explicitly imparting such information. Many faculty members believe that students come to their courses having already acquired an understanding of the process of conducting library research, or that students will somehow gain this knowledge outside of their class. Indeed, many, if not most, students are able to undertake basic research and locate resources, but the strategies they use may not be the most effective or appropriate for their development into mature scholars. In an effort to understand the research process, students will often turn to peers for guidance and advice. That students emulate faculty in turning to colleagues as a source of reliable information is perhaps not strange, but it does present challenges for librarians seeking to portray the library as the go-to place for research assistance. This might point to a need for library staff to engage with groups of students who could be trained as "peer mentors" or student research assistants, who could more easily and directly connect with the student population and vouch for the expertise of librarians as needed. If faculty could emphasize the role of librarians as colleagues and as an integral part of a broader community of scholarship including faculty and students, this might further encourage students' perception of librarians not only as assistants in the research process but as approachable authorities. Additionally, if faculty welcome and encourage librarians to seek this level of engagement and make an effort to understand what library staff are trying to accomplish in this regard, the partnership could be a fruitful one. The onus is, of course, on librarians to articulate their vision; those who sit in on classes, make regular visits to the classroom, provide library instruction, and are visible in areas where students congregate may make inroads in fostering this perception.

Our research also identified a Catch-22 for faculty who want their students to receive more comprehensive research instruction yet feel constrained by the limited time they have with students to accomplish class objectives. This conflict could be partly addressed by librarians working with faculty to better prioritize the integration of research skills training into the syllabus. Some

examples of this might include opportunities for librarians to engage with students outside of class time. For instance, an instructor might require students to meet with a librarian for an individual research consultation in preparation for a writing assignment or request that a librarian review and provide feedback to students on the quality of resources used in an annotated bibliography. Additionally, faculty members may wish to work with a librarian to organize one or more research sessions to be held outside of class time to provide more flexibility. Not all members of the instructional faculty will be open to these ideas and approaches, but librarians must continue their efforts to work in concert with faculty toward building a community that includes both library staff and students. Doing so successfully will require the establishment of new mental models among the faculty and more fully developed perceptions of the role of librarians as partners and allies in the development of students as scholars.

Communication and Change

The work reported in this volume has numerous implications for the University of Rochester Libraries and for other academic libraries and their communities of developing scholars, and we share our methods and findings in the hope that others will find ways to use them. We believe that all of us who do this kind of work should share it within our own institutions and with the larger library community through formal academic publications and conference presentations. But the sharing should not stop there. Libraries conducting these studies should also share their findings with the research participants, that is, with the students and faculty members whose academic activities we work so hard to support. The more we can build a community around these projects, the more we can foster ownership of goals and outcomes and, in turn, stimulate greater interest in future research activities. This has been our experience at the University of Rochester. Our students still speak with pride about their role in the design of the Gleason Library in 2006—it does not matter that the speakers may not have been here in 2006. Sharing library research at the institutional level also engenders respect for the library and staff, and some findings may prove to have broader application on campus. Sharing our research knits the library more closely into the community at large and provides access to the support and resources that real change requires. Real change, of course, is the object: In the end, it is most important that the library improve its own practices. The insights provided by our ethnographic research increase our chances of making good, information-based decisions and implementing changes that improve our libraries and meet the evolving needs of the people who rely on them.

Appendix 11A. ~~Ten~~ 26 Habits of Highly Successful Students

What do some students do that makes them so successful? As we worked our way through the analysis of photos, videos, maps, drawings, and more, we were struck by the habits of students who "got it." We got together to brainstorm the 10 practices that emerged time and again in our studies of undergraduates. Of course, there were more than 10, but we stopped at 26 and here they are:

1. Find friends who support your good points
2. Use a calendar
3. Find a good role model
4. Plan ahead
5. Talk to your professor
6. Love your paper topic
7. Sleep and eat well
8. Go see your TA
9. Develop your own processes
10. Find a workspace that works for you
11. Find mentors
12. Talk to your parents but don't depend on their opinions for everything
13. Use any tool that you can get your hands on
14. Organize your materials
15. Prepare the environment in which you will be writing the paper
16. Talk to librarians
17. Focus on one subject at a time
18. Get away from distraction
19. Take classes that interest you
20. Don't over commit
21. Use the writing center
22. Mine bibliographies
23. Work with professors
24. Get exercise
25. Balance work and play
26. Attend a conference

References

Abbott, A. (2008). The traditional future: A computational theory of library research. *College and Research Libraries, 69*(6), 523–545. http://crl.acrl.org/content/69/6/524.abstract.

Asher, A., Duke, L., & Green, D. (2010). The ERIAL project: Ethnographic research in Illinois academic libraries. Paper presented at the National Institute for Technology in Liberal Education Summit 2010, New Orleans, LA. Retrieved from http://www.erialproject.org/wp-content/uploads/2010/03/NITLE_summit_presentation__final_3_22_10.pdf

Bourdieu, P., Darbel, A., & Schnapper, D. (1990). *The love of art: European art museums and their public.* (C. Beattie & N. Merriman, Trans.). Stanford, CA: Stanford University.

Fredericksen, E.E. (2012). *Student IT study: University of Rochester.* Retrieved from http://www.rochester.edu/college/ctltr/Studies/UR_Student_IT_Study_2012.pdf

Head, A.J. & Eisenberg, M.B. (2011). *Balancing act: How college students manage technology while in the library during crunch time* (Project Information Literacy Research Report: "Balancing Act"). Retrieved from http://projectinfolit.org/pdfs/PIL_Fall2011_TechStudy_FullReport1.1.pdf

Martin, J. (2008). A future place for us: Results of a survey on the academic library "as a place." In J.M. Hulbert (Ed.), *Defining relevancy: Managing the new academic library* (pp. 65–84), Westport, CT: Libraries Unlimited.

Stephan, E. (2005). The academic library as place. *Mississippi Libraries, 69*(1), 3–4. Retrieved from http://www.academia.edu/563293/The_academic_library_as_place

Zweizig, D. L. (1973). *Predicting amount of library use: An empirical study of the role of the public library in the life of the adult public.* (Doctoral dissertation). ProQuest Dissertations and Theses. (302712271)

About the Authors

Nancy Fried Foster, volume editor and author of several chapters, is senior anthropologist at Ithaka S+R where she works on participatory design of library technologies and spaces. For almost 10 years, she directed anthropological research at the University of Rochester's River Campus Libraries. She has provided workshops through the American International Consortium of Academic Libraries and the Council on Library and Information Resources.

From 2008 to 2013, **Alison Bersani** served as an engineering librarian at University of Rochester's Carlson Science and Engineering Library. She has an MLIS from Syracuse University.

Solomon Blaylock is a library assistant at University of Rochester's Rush Rhees Library. He has a BA from Empire State College in art history and religious studies and is pursuing his MLS. He is a musician, performer, and committed dilettante.

Judi Briden is a digital librarian for Public Services at the University of Rochester's River Campus Libraries and subject librarian for brain and cognitive sciences, the American Sign Language program, and public health. She has participated in user research at the university since 2003, leads the libraries' discovery search group, and serves on the design team for the Web site and special projects. She earned her MLIS from the University of Texas at Austin.

Susan K. Cardinal obtained her BS in chemistry from the University of Iowa and her MLS from Syracuse University's School of Information Studies. She is the chair of the University of Rochester's River Campus Libraries' Usability Committee and likes to study how users successfully interact with technology.

Cynthia Carlton is head of University of Rochester's River Campus Libraries' Applications Group. She holds a degree in information technology from Rochester Institute of Technology and specializes in system administration and IT security. She is passionate about learning and teaching new trends in technology.

Katie Clark is the associate director for Public Services and Collection Development at University of Rochester's River Campus Libraries. She contributed to two earlier books on user research done all, or in part, at the River Campus Libraries: *Studying Students* and *Scholarly Practice, Participatory Design and the eXtensible Catalog*.

Nora Dimmock is a subject librarian for film and media studies and digital media studies. She has an MLS from the University at Buffalo (SUNY) and is pursuing an EdD in higher education leadership at the University of Rochester's Warner School of Education. As the director of the Digital Humanities Center, she works closely with faculty members in modern languages and cultures, history, English, linguistics, and other academic departments to develop new modes of scholarship to extend teaching and learning beyond traditional print media.

149

Sarada George has been a staff member at the University of Rochester's Carlson Science and Engineering Library for over 20 years. Technology has changed steadily during that time, but she feels that students seem to be much the same. When not at the library, she is deeply involved in Balkan music and dance.

Kenn Harper is a recently retired science librarian with specialties in biology and laser fusion. He has an MS in Zoology and an MLIS from the University of Michigan.

LeRoy (Lee) LaFleur is the head of the Reference Department at University of Rochester's Rush Rhees Library and the subject librarian for anthropology. He holds a bachelor's degree in sociology from Michigan State University, a master's degree in library and information studies from the University of Wisconsin-Madison, and a master's in organization development and knowledge management from George Mason University's School of Public Policy.

Sarah Sexstone is a member of the Acquisitions Department at the University of Rochester's Rush Rhees Library where she is head of the Finance Unit. She began her library career in technical services at Marymount Manhattan College's Shanahan Library. She earned her MLS from the University at Buffalo (SUNY).

Marcy Strong is head of the Metadata Creation and Enrichment Unit at the University of Rochester's River Campus Libraries. She previously worked at Binghamton University (SUNY) and has an MSIS from the University at Albany (SUNY). Although she happily spends most of her time cataloging print monographs and digital materials, she relished the opportunity to work directly with students on this project.

Mari Tsuchiya is a senior library assistant at the Reference Department of the University of Rochester's Rush Rhees Library. She manages the library's online course pages and organizes special events such as the Human Library and Banned Books Read-Out. She was educated in Japan and taught Japanese language at Choate Rosemary Hall in Connecticut and Kenwood Academy in Chicago before coming to the Rush Rhees Library. She recently finished her MLS at the University at Buffalo (SUNY).